D0731633

SECONDARY
STARTERS AND
PLENARIES

Ready-to-use activities for teaching any subject

By Kate Brown

BLOOMSBURY

LONDON • NEW DELHI • NEW YORK • SYDNEY

Revised Edition Published 2013 by Bloomsbury Education
Bloomsbury Publishing plc
50 Bedford Square, London, WC1B 3DP

www.bloomsbury.com

9781408193570

© Kate Brown

First Published 2009 by Continuum International Publishing Group

A CIP record for this publication is available from the British Library.

All rights reserved. No part of this publication may be reproduced
in any form or by any means – graphic, electronic, or mechanical, including
photocopying, recording, taping or information storage or retrieval systems –
without the prior permission in writing of the publishers.

10 9 8 7 6 5 4 3 2 1

Typeset by Fakenham Prepress Solutions, Fakenham, Norfolk, NR21 8NN

Printed and bound by CPI Group (UK) Ltd, Croydon, CR0 4YY

This book is produced using paper that is made from wood grown in
managed, sustainable forests. It is natural, renewable and recyclable.
The logging and manufacturing processes conform to the environmental
regulations of the country of origin.

To Betty Anderson and all those who keep learning

Contents

Section 4: Game show 61

Section 5: Figure it out 87

Section 6: Physical 113

Section 7: Reflect on your learning 123

Acknowledgements

I would like to thank all the teachers who have, over the years, contributed to the ideas brought together in this book, whether they taught me as a school student, trainee, supervisee, colleague or friend.

About this book

Why starters and plenaries?

The first few minutes of a lesson are hugely important. In that five or ten minutes students can be 'switched on' and hooked into the lesson, or glaze over and 'zone out'. They can get a clear idea of what to expect from the lesson and the teacher, or start the main activity confused. And they quickly get a sense of what you expect from them.

The final few minutes of a lesson are equally crucial. Students can tie together what they have learned, and consider how it fits with what they already know, or they can be left with ideas 'hanging' as the lesson fizzles out. They can reflect on how they did in the lesson, and what they could do to improve, or leave none the wiser about how to move forward next lesson.

As a result, the activities that you plan for the start of the lesson – the starter – and for the end of the lesson – the plenary – are as important as the main activity of the lesson. Not only that, their contribution to good lesson structure is widely recognised and promoted through Ofsted feedback and in teacher training courses.

What makes a good starter or plenary?

Good starters and good plenaries have a lot in common with each other, and also a lot in common with any kind of good teaching activity. They incorporate several, if not all, of the following features:

- *Clear aim.* The teacher must be clear about how the activity will contribute to students' learning, and how this fits with the aims of the unit, scheme of work and/or exam specifications.

- *Clear instructions.* While keeping 'teacher talk' to a minimum, students need to know what they will be doing.

- *Engagement.* Students should be interested in and curious about the material or the style of the activity. They should be motivated for the current, or future, lesson.

- *Pace.* Students should start or finish their learning briskly, giving them (and the teacher) a sense of the pace at which they need to operate, a sense of purpose and of moving forward.

- *Participation.* The activities should involve every student, not just the two or three who always put up their hand to answer a question.

- *Access.* Activities where even the most basic elements or questions are pitched at the more able members of the group exclude students. The whole class should be able to access the material and make their own contribution.

- *Challenge.* Students should be encouraged to think for themselves and build on what they know. Each student should be challenged and stretched – so the activity must allow differentiated outcomes.

- *Creativity.* These short activities are a chance to try new things, explore a topic in an unexpected way, and to be imaginative and sometimes playful.

- *Variety.* Activities should not follow a set, repetitive, pattern. They should vary from lesson to lesson, based on different stimuli, requiring different types of responses, developing different skills, and using different teaching styles: visual, auditory, kinaesthetic.

- *Assessment for learning.* Whether in the form of informal comments on students' oral contributions, answering students' questions or peer marking of a short test, starters and plenaries often include opportunities for the teacher to assess the learning of the class as a whole, or of individual students. The information gained by the teacher about student progress can help inform the style, pace and content of subsequent teaching; and students can develop their understanding through the feedback they receive.

- *Reflection.* Students should have time to consider how their learning fits into a topic, how the topic is relevant to other subjects and their broader lives, and the progress they have made and can make in the future.

The aim of this book

Of course, there is a lot more than effective starters and plenaries for the time-pressed teacher to consider in the planning of a good lesson. What can you do to ensure smooth transitions between activities? What are the learning objectives for the lesson? How long will each activity/element of the lesson take? Do you have all the resources and equipment that you need? Are there any behaviour issues you need to consider?

In the midst of all that, it is easy to overlook starters and plenaries. They can be forgotten altogether in a flurry of uniform checks, register-taking, collecting homework, setting homework, packing away and tidying the classroom. Or you can easily get 'stuck in a rut', using the same few ideas repeatedly, and falling back too often on the question, 'So, who can tell me what we learned last lesson?'

There are times when a starter or plenary activity specific to a subject and tailored for a particular topic comes easily to hand and works extremely well. That might be getting students to physically represent atoms in solids, liquids and gases in a chemistry lesson, watching a news clip on the day of an earthquake in geography, or analysing a source in history. There are many ready-made subject specific starter and plenary activities to buy or find on the internet.

However, it can often be difficult to find an activity that exactly fits the stage of a topic you have reached, the angle you have approached the material from, the size of your group or the ability of your students. Simply 'cutting and pasting' such activities into your lesson can lead to unclear progression from previous learning or to the main activity of the lesson, and confused students. You can adapt such activities to fit your lesson, but sometimes, by the time you have done so, you might as well have started from scratch.

This book offers a different approach to starters and plenaries. It outlines 50 ideas which can be used flexibly and easily by teachers to keep the start and end of their lessons fresh, pacey and engaging. Rather than being content driven, they are activity based: the descriptions provided on these pages focus on the format and style of the activities themselves. The result is 50 activity 'shells', which can be easily and quickly adapted for any lesson by 'slotting in' relevant subject specific content. Taken as a whole, this book aims to provide a toolkit for teachers, a suite of tools which they can select from to start and end any lesson, or dip into when they are in need of inspiration.

How to use this book

Each activity outlined in this book can be used for a starter or a plenary. To help you navigate the activities, they have been categorized into different groups depending on their focus or style, each representing a different section of the book:

1. *In your own words (or pictures)*. These are activities which encourage students to summarize, order, manipulate or illustrate their learning using their own words or images.

2. *Questioning*. Questioning is a hugely powerful and important tool in teaching, and these activities offer a range of different approaches to the use of the question.

3. *Key words*. This section contains activities which support students in defining, learning and using key words.

4. *Game show*. Based on well-known television, radio or board games, these activities use a familiar format and sense of competitiveness to engage students.

5. *Figure it out*. These are activities which include a mystery, puzzle or challenge that students have to unravel or complete.

6. *Physical*. Activities which incorporate movement – great activities for after lunch, Friday afternoons and for kinaesthetic learners.

7. *Reflect on your learning.* This final section contains activities which encourage students to reflect on the way in which they learn: what have they understood, what have they done well, and how can they improve?

Below is a guide to the format of each activity, explaining the key features and purpose of each element.

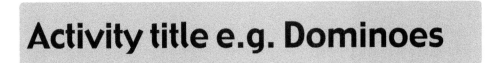

Activity title e.g. Dominoes

What's the idea? At the top of the page you will find an explanation of the activity, including what preparation is needed, what students will need to do and the materials needed. The idea is that each activity is very flexible, and easily adapted to suit you and your students' needs, so this core explanation is kept fairly short.

Variations

Having introduced the basic recipe, this section suggests ingredients you could add in or take away, and how to cater for different tastes. A range of different ideas is included to help you adapt the activity to fit your lessons. Experiment with these variations to provide variety and work out what works when.

Examples

Topic e.g. Tectonic processes

For each activity, one or more examples are included. In each example box title is the topic of the example, and the subject and level are also specified:

Subject: e.g. Geography, Maths
Level: e.g. Key Stage 3, Key Stage 4

In some cases the 'teacher talk' at the start of the activity is outlined. In others, an example of student work is used as an illustration.

The main aim of these examples is not that they be used directly by the reader; they are intended to help better explain the activity, and illustrate the ways in which it could be used. Of course, if the example given fits your lesson and group well, then feel free to use it or adapt it.

As already mentioned, good starters and good plenaries have a lot in common. The majority of the activities in this book have been, and can be, adapted for use either at the start or end of the lesson. Of course, while starters and plenaries can be similar in many ways, they also have different emphases. A starter is a more likely point in the lesson to introduce new learning and 'hook' students into a particular topic. Plenaries can be more obvious times to celebrate achievement and reflect on progress – though this is certainly not a hard-and-fast rule. As a result, some of the activities described more obviously lend themselves to being either starter or plenary activities.

As the page layout opposite indicates, a full explanation of how to use each activity with your students is included. However, there are two key factors which are important in the effective use of many of these starters and plenaries. You will find them cropping up repeatedly over the pages of this book, and they are worth a further word here.

Clear timing

Starters and plenaries should be what their name suggests – confined to the very beginning and end of the lesson. Sticking to timings sets or keeps a brisk pace, and prevents running into the time needed for the main lesson activity. Sharing timings with students ('You have three minutes to …') helps students work to the pace you are setting, and to effectively manage the time they are given. Different teachers time activities in different ways. You may simply tell students at the start how long they have, or the time you will finish, and then warn them again just before the time is up. Others use a stopwatch, or a virtual stopwatch, so that each student can see exactly how much time they have left. Good timers on the internet include:

- www.teachit.co.uk/custom_content/timer/clock3.html. Adjust to any length of time, and select your preferred sound to indicate time-up.

- www.classtools.net/main_area/timer.htm. Choose from a range of timers – perhaps the *Pink Panther* at 2 minutes 39 second timer, or the *Indiana Jones* theme tune at 5 minutes 14 seconds.

Feedback

Many, but by no means all, of the starters and plenaries involve feedback at the end of the activity: students put forward their ideas, answers and suggestions, and the teacher, or their peers, correct, respond and comment. It is an element of the activity that allows you to assess students' learning and help them to develop their ideas. Feedback draws the activity to a close and links it to the main activity of the lesson or the next lesson. Students share their learning, and can assess their own understanding in relation to that of their peers. As a result, it is important to leave sufficient time for this significant element of the activity, and for students to expect this time for you, and them, to reflect on their answers. Questions to prompt and structure feedback might include:

- Who would be willing to share their answer?

- Why did you choose that option?

- Was it a close-run thing, or did you nearly choose another answer?

- Are there any potential problems with this suggestion?

- What is the definition of the word you gave as an answer?

- How does the answer link to what you have been learning about?

Section 1
In your own words (or pictures)

Everything you know

At the start of a new topic, explain the title of the new unit of work, and then ask students to write down everything they already know. Set a clear time frame, and then lead feedback of students' ideas to the class.

Students can use any format to organize what they know: full sentences; bullet points; spider diagrams; mind maps. This can be a good context in which to talk to them about different styles of ordering and presenting material and what works for them.

This activity allows students to draw on their existing learning before building on it, and gives you a sense of what students already know so that you can pitch your lessons effectively.

Variations

- Repeat the activity at the end of the unit and then ask students to compare the two sets of information. What do they think are the most significant things they have learned?

- This activity can also work well at the end of a unit, perhaps as part of revision for an end-of-unit assessment. Give students time at home or in the lesson to read through their notes, and then ask them to write down what they know on the topic. This activity is much more effective if you emphasize the structure of what they know, the key ideas and how they are linked, rather than every single fact and detail. As mentioned above, talk to students about mind mapping and how they think their knowledge can be ordered and subdivided under different headings.

Example

Glaciation

Subject: Geography
Level: Key Stage 3

A student's glaciation mind map:

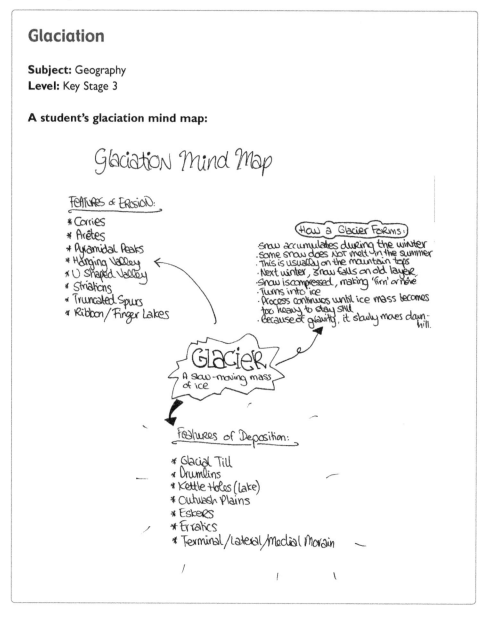

Glaciation Mind Map

FEATURES of EROSION:
* Corries
* Arêtes
* Pyramidal Peaks
* Hanging Valley
* U Shaped Valley
* Striations
* Truncated Spurs
* Ribbon / Finger Lakes

How a Glacier Forms:
. Snow accumulates during the winter
. Some snow does not melt in the summer
. This is usually on the mountain tops
. Next winter, snow falls on old layer
. Snow is compressed, making 'firn' or névé
. Turns into ice
. Process continues until ice mass becomes too heavy to stay still
. Because of gravity, it slowly moves downhill.

GLACIER
A slow-moving mass of ice

Features of Deposition:
* Glacial Till
* Drumlins
* Kettle Holes (Lake)
* Outwash Plains
* Eskers
* Erratics
* Terminal / Lateral / Medial Morain

List three things

Ask students to write down three things they have learned in this lesson (as a plenary) or in the previous lesson (as a starter). They can list more than three if they want, but no fewer. Bullet points are fine. Give them a clear time limit, and when they have finished ask for volunteers (or select students) to each share one item from their list.

Asking students to recap what they have learned is probably the most straightforward way of concluding a lesson, or opening one. Formatting it in this way is a crisper approach than an open-ended 'What have you learned?' This activity is also a really useful assessment for learning tool – students are able to reflect on their learning relative to others, and you can assess what they have learned to help you pitch the lesson.

Variations

• Give students mini-whiteboards to write on as a clear demarcation of this part of the lesson. Students are often more confident about writing on whiteboards – mistakes can simply be rubbed out.

• Change the instruction from 'Write down three things you learned this lesson' to 'Write down three things your partner learned this lesson'. Students may find it easier to reflect orally in pairs before they write.

• Compare what students write to the learning objectives which you displayed at the start of the lesson.

Example

North Indian classical music

Subject: Music
Level: Key Stage 3

At the end of a lesson introducing North Indian classical music, students were asked to write down three new things they had learned. One student made the following list:

- Raga = melody

- Religious music

- Over 2,000 years old

Summarize...

Start by asking for a summary, in five sentences, of 'What you've learned this lesson'. If it is possible, give a clearer instruction: 'Summarize the specific concept/issue/idea/process you covered this lesson' (delete as applicable/insert details). It needs to be exactly five sentences, though these can vary in length – so students need to include enough detail, but also summarize rather than simply regurgitate. To elucidate the key points, they will really need to think about what they have covered and what is important. You can do this stage with, or without, books or notes. As always, provide a clear time frame (perhaps three or five minutes depending on the group and the difficultly of the topic).

Next step: students choose five words which, between them, sum up the five sentence summary. You can ask that these form a short sentence, or they can be five key words which do not sit together grammatically. Give students a shorter time frame for this step. Finally, students must pick one single word – the word that they think best sums up the idea or topic. This must not be in the title/name of what they are summarizing. Finish the activity by asking students to feed back their ideas for one or more of the steps. Why do they think the words or word they chose are the best summary?

Variations

- If some students find the first step, summarizing in five sentences, too difficult, ask other students to share their summaries. Provide feedback on these to the class, to help all students move forward to the second step.

- You can use this activity as a longer game at the end of a unit when you have several processes/ideas to revise. Write these on pieces of card and distribute one to each pair or group of students (for example: 'Ox-bow lake formation'; 'Rapid formation'; 'Waterfall formation'; 'Meander formation'). Ask each group to summarize their process in five sentences, and then to feed back their summary to the whole class. Next, take the cards back in, shuffle and redistribute. Having listened to the five-sentence definitions, students now have a shorter time to pick five words to describe their new process. Without telling the class what their new process is, each group then shares their five words. The rest of the class must guess, from this summary, what the process is. Shuffle the cards again, and repeat: this time each group must give a one-word description, and the whole class must guess their process.

- Played as a party game, this activity has a final step, in which you must 'act out' (with no words) the name of the famous figure you have selected. This can be applied to this classroom activity too – to memorable effect!

Example

The role of enzymes in the digestive system

Subject: Biology
Level: Key Stage 3

Five sentences:
Perhaps: 'Enzymes are proteins that break large molecules into small molecules. Different enzymes do different things, e.g. carbohydrase or amylase enzymes break down starch into sugar and protease enzymes break down proteins into amino acids.

Carbohydrates are digested in the mouth, stomach and small intestine, starting with enzymes in saliva. Proteins are digested in the stomach (helped by stomach acid) and the small intestine. Digestion of fat in the small intestine is helped by bile, made in the liver, which breaks downs fat into small droplets, which lipase enzymes can work on more easily.'

Five words:
Maybe: 'Different enzymes break different molecules', or 'Enzymes help digestion, break molecules', or 'Enzymes, proteins, break, help, digestion'.

One word:
Perhaps: 'Break' or 'Digestion'.

Visually represent

This is basically a visual version of the 'Summarize...' activity on page 6, good for the visual learners among your students. Ask students to sketch a representation of what they have learned. The emphasis should be on the information that the illustration puts across, not on immaculate presentation.

You may want to vary your instructions, depending on what you have covered. If you have been learning about a key process, students might design a simple diagram to represent the stages. If you have been covering an issue or idea, they might design a symbol which visually sums up the content. In either case, their challenge is to get as much information into their drawing as possible, but using as few words as they can – they will need to be imaginative!

Variations

- Instead of drawing in their book or on their mini-whiteboard, like the rest of the class, ask one student to work on the main classroom whiteboard. This means, for the feedback, that you will have one example everyone can comment on. How well does the illustration convey information about the topic?

- For an extra challenge, hand out a particular size/shape of paper on which students must draw, maybe a circle, or oblong. If you use coloured paper, this can also produce eye-catching results for wall displays.

Examples

The Berlin blockade

Subject: History
Level: Key Stage 4

The diagram on the next page summarizes the following facts about the Berlin Blockade:

- Where Berlin is geographically located in Germany.

- That Berlin and Germany were split into four zones, under the control of the USSR, Britain, France and America, and roughly where these zones were.

- That Britain, France and Germany joined their zones into a new country called West Germany.

- That in June 1948 Stalin cut off all rail and road links to West Berlin.

- That, in response, 275,000 planes transported goods into West Berlin.

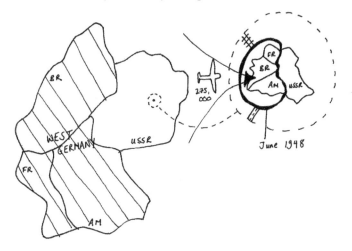

Energy

Subject: Physics
Level: Key Stage 3

The symbol below is one student's representation of different types of renewable energy:

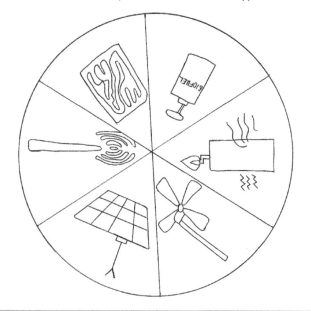

Annotate

This activity is a cross between the 'summarize' and 'visually represent' activities on the previous pages. Hand out a picture, photo, or graph. This figure should be photocopied in the middle of a sheet of paper, or stuck into the middle of the page in students' books, so that there is plenty of room to annotate.

Explain to students that the idea is to add as many labels as possible to the picture, so that someone coming fresh to the topic would understand what is going on. From every feature of the image or graph they should draw an arrow to the side of the page. At the side of the page they should write exactly what the arrow is pointing to and what that feature shows or why it is important.

Variations

- For added challenge, or if students have already been working from a diagram or graph, ask students to sketch the figure before they annotate, either from memory, or with the aid of their book.

- Set a precise number of annotations, or a limit on the length of the labels, so that students have to think really carefully about what they will include.

- If you have access to computers, students can complete their annotations on screen rather than by hand.

- Ask students to find their own picture at home, from a magazine or printed from the internet, and use these as a starter for the next lesson. For example, students could bring in a photograph of a glacier, and start the lesson by labelling as many features of the glacier and the surrounding landscape as they can.

- To help with feedback at the end of this activity, or to use it solely as an oral activity, project an image at the front of the room and ask students to come up and point to different features on the board, giving a brief description – an oral annotation.

Examples

Lord of the Flies

Subject: English Literature
Level: Key Stage 3

Give students a simple sketch of a tall, thin boy, or perhaps ask them to draw a stick man in the centre of an A4 page. Project or give them a copy of the list below, which gives information about the character Jack in *Lord of the Flies*. Ask them to annotate their drawing with the information, to build up a visual profile of Jack's appearance and character.

- He is tall and thin.

- He has red hair.

- He has a 'crumpled face'.

- He has blue eyes.

- He can sing – he used to be leader of a choir.

- He is proud, arrogant and hungry for power.

- He is obsessed with hunting.

- He wears a mask which helps him hunt.

Each piece of information should be written around the stick man and joined by an arrow to a relevant part of the body. For example, an arrow would point from the words 'Blue eyes' to his eyes; from 'Red hair' to his hair (which could also be coloured in red). Students could add details to the drawing to help them annotate, for example a knife in Jack's hand for the annotation 'Obsessed with hunting'.

Rather than giving students a list of Jack's characteristics that you have collated, as a starter challenge them to complete the annotation with any details they can remember from reading the text. Alternatively, as the main activity of the lesson ask students to read through the text and collate their own list, and then use this to complete an annotation as a plenary.

Hitler's rise to power

Subject: History
Level: Key Stage 4

Ask GCSE History students to draw a vertical line down the side of a page, and divide it into five parts, labelling the divisions 1935, 1936, 1937, 1938, and 1939. Ask them to place Hitler's aggressive actions, which eventually led to the Second World War, along the timeline. They should try to be as accurate as possible, indicating through their placement on the line the year, season and even month of each event. You can make it easier by giving them the following list and asking them to place them along the timeline:

- Rearmament.

- Remilitarization of the Rhineland.

- *Anschluss* with Austria.

- Annexation of the Sudetenland.

- Invasion of Czechoslovakia.

- Invasion of Poland.

Mnemonics

Mnemonics are memory devices. They can be names, words, rhymes, sayings or even pictures. There are many well-known mnemonics, often used by teachers – for example, '**N**ever **E**at **S**hredded **W**heat' for points of the compass, or '**R**ichard **O**f **Y**ork **G**ave **B**attle **I**n **V**ain' for the colours of the rainbow. For a quick starter or plenary, challenge students to create their own mnemonic for a word, list or concept.

Variations

- Lists of names or terms work well for creating 'phrase' mnemonics, replacing each term with a word with the same starting letter, to create a sentence. For example, the planets (Mercury, Venus, Earth, Mars, Jupiter, Saturn, Uranus, and Neptune) might become '**M**any **V**ast **E**arthlings **M**unch **J**uicy **S**trawberries **U**nder **N**ets'.

- Mnemonics do not have to follow first letters, they can be any short rhyme or saying that helps you remember a rule. So, for example, Chemistry students studying the periodic table might create a saying to help them remember that the rows are called periods, and the columns are groups (perhaps: 'In this period we went a long way to remembering the elements, now we'll go down in groups to lunch').

- Mnemonics can also be used to memorize numbers. For example, 'How I wish I could calculate pi', gives the first seven digits of pi (the number of letters in each word tells you the digit, so: 3.141592).

Examples

> ### Classification system
>
> **Subject:** Biology
> **Level:** Key Stage 3
>
> Challenge students to create a mnemonic for the classification system: Kingdom, Phylum, Class, Order, Family, Genus, Species. You could give them an example to get them thinking: '**K**ing **P**urchases **C**lassy **O**bjects **F**rom **G**iant **S**uperstore'.

Map skills

Subject: Geography
Level: Key Stage 3

Students created the mnemonics shown below to help them remember that lines of longitude run North–South, and lines of latitude run East–West.

My cat latti is fat but my cat longi is tall.

Latitude is an elephant.
Longitude is a giraffe.

What do you say to that?

In this activity students have to script a response to a question or statement. Set the scene for them: did they hear the remark in the queue for a bus or in the corridor at school? Was it made by another student or by a teacher or other adult? Then tell them what was said – it could be a factually incorrect statement, or a controversial viewpoint.

Give students a set amount of time, individually or in pairs, to craft their answer. They need to set the person straight, or put across their own viewpoint. They need to be factually correct. However, they also need to think about making sure the other person listens to them: that means being clear and engaging, but also polite. Finally, they need to think about pitching their answer to their audience: how can they explain their answer so that a six-year-old understands? Or their head teacher?

Variations

• Rather than using a question or remark as the stimulus, ask students to write an explanation of a concept or idea for use in a specific context or for a specific audience. Asking them to explain the idea as though it was for their little brother or sister works well. They need to really understand the process or concept to put it into simple and clear language. Alternatives include writing an explanation for an older person (who might not be technologically fluent), or for the audience of a radio chat show (who may have little subject-specific understanding).

Examples

Consumer laws and standards

Subject: Design and Technology
Level: Key Stage 4

Ask students to imagine that they were chatting to one of their friends about shopping at the weekend. The friend says, 'I bought this really great shirt at the weekend, but when I got it home, it was the wrong size. It said on the packet that it was my size, so I took it back to the shop. But the shop owner said I should have checked more carefully before I bought it. It's my fault that I've got a shirt that doesn't fit!'

Drawing on what they have learned about consumer law, ask students to script what they would say to their friend to try and put him right. The first time you use this activity, or to support students who are finding it harder, tell them that a good answer would include reference to:

- The Trade Descriptions Act 1968.

- What your friend should expect the retailer to offer in this situation.

- What your friend should do if they feel their consumer rights are breached.

Genes and inheritance

Subject: Biology
Level: Key Stage 4

Teacher introduction: 'Your little sister is playing in the sitting room while your family watch the news. She hears an item about research into Cystic Fibrosis, a genetically inherited illness. She knows you are studying genetics at school so she asks you, "What is a gene?" You have five minutes in pairs to write an answer she will understand. You can use your textbooks and your work from last lesson'.

Local government

Subject: Citizenship
Level: Key Stage 3

'What has local government got to do with me? It's just a load of old people in suits. Why should I bother voting?'

Ask students to prepare an answer to this question to try and persuade the speaker that they should vote in a local election. To help students target their answer you could decide on the age/sex/occupation of the speaker, or let students create a character of their own.

Section 2
Questioning

Questions...with a twist

Questions from teacher to students and from students to teacher are a part of every lesson. Asking questions ('Which side of the graph is the x-axis?' or 'What does ISP stand for?') are an easy link to previous learning or to assess what has been learned in a lesson. However, while questioning is a vital part of differentiation, assessment for learning and participation, it is easy to fall into a pattern of only engaging those students quick to put their hand up. Varying the format in which you question at the start and end of lessons can be fun and motivating and help get all of your class involved, developing a deeper understanding.

Some simple ideas for questioning with a twist are outlined in the section below, with the variations and examples rolled in. You will find other ideas in this section and also in Section 4, 'Game show'.

Lucky dip

Write your questions on pieces of paper beforehand and fold or scrunch them up, put them in a container (jam jar, hat, mug), and ask for volunteers or pick students to select and answer a question. You can allow students one chance to pick again if they do not know the answer, which gives more control to the student.

Example

Rock weathering

Subject: Chemistry
Level: Key Stage 3

Questions for your question-jar might include:

- What is weathering?

- Can you name a type of physical weathering?

- How can plants contribute to biological weathering?

- Why is normal rainwater slightly acidic?

- Can you name a type of rock that is easily chemically weathered?

Pick a card

Produce two stacks of cards numbered 1 to 30 (or 1 to x, where x is the number of students in your class). Distribute a card to each student. Shuffle the second pack and then turn over the first card. Find out which student has the same number. Ask that student a question. Repeat, shuffling the pack in between so that a student can get asked a question more than once. This can be done with playing cards, but you need to remove surplus cards (perhaps take out one or more suits).

Example

Reading non-fiction texts

Subject: English language
Level: Key Stage 4

Distribute a short non-fiction text to students who are familiar with analysing such texts. Give them time to read it through. Select students, using the card system outlined above, to answer the following questions and explain their answers:

- What is this text?

- Who is it aimed at?

- What is the text trying to get you to do?

- What can you say about the use of language?

- What can you say about the style of writing?

- What can you say about the tone of the extract?

- Is the information fact or opinion?

Can't say 'Yes' or 'No'

Explain the key rule – that whatever the question they are asked, students cannot reply with the answers 'Yes' or 'No'. The idea is to encourage students to give longer, more in-depth answers. You can arm a student with a 'buzzer' to sound if they hear 'Yes' or 'No' in the answer. You might want to display on the board some alternative ways to start an answer. This activity works well for questions that are asking for opinion.

Example

Jane Eyre

Subject: English Literature
Level: Key Stage 4

Open a lesson by asking students the following questions. They can't say 'Yes' or 'No', but they could start 'Through her writing Charlotte Brontë...', 'Jane is certainly...' or 'To a certain extent...'

- Do you feel sympathy for Jane Eyre's character?

- Do you admire Jane's character?

- Does Jane face any difficulties?

- Does Jane always do what is right?

'Why?'

'Why?' is a really powerful question and asking it repeatedly can help students develop a line of argument. Begin with an opening question, which starts 'Why ... ?' When a student gives an answer, respond with the same question: 'Why?' Repeat the question until the student has developed his or her explanation as far as possible.

Example

The world as a global community

Subject: Citizenship
Level: Key Stage 4

Open with the question, 'Where are the clothes you are wearing made?' After looking at their labels, students will likely produce a list of countries including Vietnam, India, China, Indonesia, mostly 'developing countries'. Ask why: why are so many of our clothes produced in these countries when we are capable of making them in the UK? Answers might include 'They can make them cheaper', 'Cheap labour' etc. Again ask why: 'Why can they make them cheaper?', 'Why is labour cheap?' Students may answer 'Because there are fewer rules and regulations about health and safety, the environment', 'Because the employees can be paid less'. You can keep going in this way, each time leading students to a deeper level of understanding on an issue.

Questioning: a team sport

You can add a competitive edge to questioning in class by dividing students into teams, giving a point or points for each question answered correctly, and keeping a tally of each team's score. The most straightforward way to do this is to split the class into two teams, directing your questions to one team and then the other, and allocating one point for each question answered correctly. You could appoint a student as score-keeper, writing the score down on the board. You can work on a 'First hand up' basis within each team, ask teams to confer and give their answers via an appointed spokesperson (works well with small groups, but less so in larger ones), or pick a student to whom you are addressing the question.

Variations

- Vary the scoring according to how hard the question is. So 'Who were the Vietcong?' might score one point in a GCSE History group, and 'What month and year did the TET offensive take place?' might be worth two. You can also vary the points you award depending on the quality of the answer, and offer bonus points for extra information, for example 'What is teleworking? A bonus point for naming a company that uses teleworkers'. You can take points off for wrong answers, though this can discourage students who are unsure of the answer from having a go.

- A potentially more relevant and motivating method of varying the score with the difficulty of the question or the quality of the answer is to draw on the scoring methods used in sports. An easy question could be one cricket run, a more difficult question two or three. Or, in ascending degrees of question difficulty, correct answers could win a red ball (one point), yellow ball (two points), green ball (three points), brown ball (four points) etc. Alternatively, a very high quality answer could score six runs, or a five-point blue ball, as opposed to a very simple answer which scores one run or a red ball.

- Another way of reducing the predictability of a round of questioning is to vary the points available at random. Prepare a pack of cards by removing the higher scoring cards, leaving ace to four or five in all suits. Select a student from one of the teams to pick a card. The points available for the question you then ask them are the number on the card.

- Sticking to one point per question, tennis scoring is a novel system to pick: 'Love', '15', '30', '40', 'Game' for each successive question answered correctly. Alternatively, you could encourage 'rallies' of questions and answers, only giving a point (to the opposite team) when someone drops the ball by getting a question wrong.

- There are lots of pair and team games available on the internet based on questioning. For example, the website www.juicygeography.co.uk has a 'rivers penalty shootout' and www.schoolhistory.co.uk has a bank of teacher-created quizzes in various styles.

Examples

Renaissance medicine

Subject: History
Level: Key Stage 4

The table below gives the start of a quiz on Renaissance medicine. The questions were addressed to the two teams alternately, and the answers given are also noted. The last column lists the number of 'cricket' runs that were awarded to the team, related to how relevant and detailed their answer was.

Table I

Team	Question	Answer	Runs awarded
A	What did Vesalius discover?	Vessels in your testicles	I
B	What did Vesalius publish?	*The Fabric of the Human Body*, which had amazing illustrations	3
A	Where did William Harvey train and work?	England	I
B	What did Harvey prove about blood?	He wrote a book which scientifically proved that blood circulates around the body	2
A	How did Thomas Sydenham think diseases were caused?	He thought they were caused by 'atmospheres', but he did think that doctors should visit their patients, not the other way round, which was some progress in stopping the spread of disease	4
B	How was syphilis thought to be caused at the time?	By God	I

Religious festivals

Subject: RE
Level: Key Stage 3

Below is a set of questions testing students' knowledge on religious festivals. They are coded according to the 'snooker ball' they are worth. Ask each team a question in turn, selecting a 'colour' at random, or letting them choose the colour they want to take a shot at:

Red ball questions – one point:

- What do Christians celebrate at Christmas?

- What is the proper name of the Hindu festival of lights?

- Why do Christians eat Easter eggs at Easter?

- What word, beginning with F, is another name for a celebration of a special occasion?

- What do Jewish people ask of God on the solemn day of Yom Kippur?

- What miraculously burned in the Jewish temple for eight days and is remembered at Hanukkah?

Yellow ball question – two points:

- What is the name of the Hindu festival where people throw coloured powder, and what are they celebrating?

Green ball question – three points:

- What do Muslims celebrate at Eid Ul Adha, and name one way they celebrate?

Brown ball question – four points:

- What three stages of whose life are remembered at the festival of Wesak?

True or false?

Read out, write up on the board or project a number of statements to students, which relate to the learning in the lesson or in the previous lesson. Ask them to identify and write down whether each statement is true or false.

Some of the questioning strategies mentioned so far encourage students to develop and explain their answers – for example, where answering 'Yes' or 'No' is not allowed, or where a higher score is given for a fuller answer. 'True or false' does the opposite – no explanation is required (though can be discussed in the feedback), allowing a quick-fire round of several questions. This can provide a snappy way to start or end a lesson.

Variations

- Distribute mini-whiteboards for students to write their answers on. Project or read statements one at a time, and for each one ask students to write a large T or F on their whiteboard and hold it up. You can give a time limit within which every student must be holding up their board (see 'Show me', page 120).

Example

Chemical reactions

Subject: Chemistry
Level: Key Stage 3

Chemical reactions: true or false?

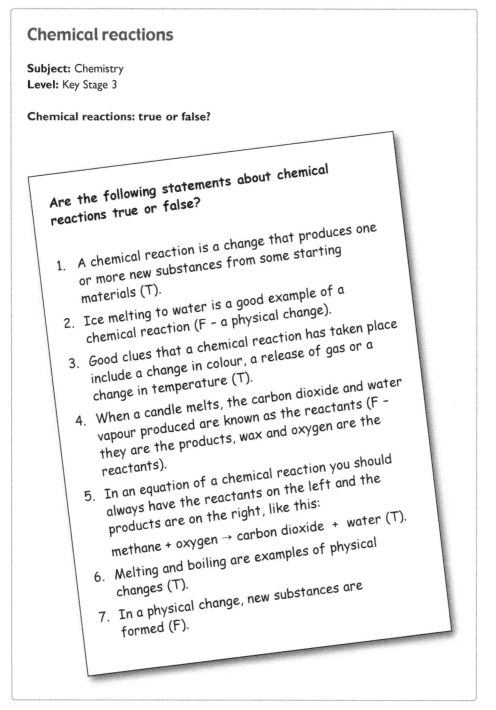

Are the following statements about chemical reactions true or false?

1. A chemical reaction is a change that produces one or more new substances from some starting materials (T).

2. Ice melting to water is a good example of a chemical reaction (F - a physical change).

3. Good clues that a chemical reaction has taken place include a change in colour, a release of gas or a change in temperature (T).

4. When a candle melts, the carbon dioxide and water vapour produced are known as the reactants (F - they are the products, wax and oxygen are the reactants).

5. In an equation of a chemical reaction you should always have the reactants on the left and the products are on the right, like this:

   methane + oxygen → carbon dioxide + water (T).

6. Melting and boiling are examples of physical changes (T).

7. In a physical change, new substances are formed (F).

What would you ask me?

This, and the ideas over the next few pages, get students asking questions instead of, or as well as, answering them. In this case, you, the teacher, will be answering the questions. Take the character of a figure that students are learning about – a named individual (a political leader, well-known scientist, or historical figure) or an 'average' person (for example, a soldier, a member of an electorate, a patient).

Give students a time limit in which to write down questions they want to ask you. You can either collect in all the questions and pick them from a hat, or select students to pose questions.

This activity works best, in terms of engaging and holding students' attention, if you get into the character you choose. Bring props (items of clothing, objects), project photographs of your setting, and introduce yourself. You will obviously want to pick a character about which you know, or can give a reasonable 'guesstimate' to most questions. If a student poses a particularly specific or obscure question, and inevitably they will, then try: 'I'm being briefed on that later today'; 'I've not been directly involved in that side of things'; 'That's classified information' ...

As well as providing answers to specific questions students are interested in, you can use your answers to cover the material you want to cover, drawing in issues and topics students' questions have not directly touched on.

Variations

- For a shorter starter or plenary, ask students to write down one question they would like to ask a chosen figure they have been studying. You can run feedback immediately, using students' questions to assess how well they have understood the significance of the chosen figure, or you can ask students to try and find out the answer to their question for homework.

Examples

World War One trench warfare

Subject: History
Level: Key Stage 3

Give students a chance to ask a young soldier what life was really like on the Western Front. Choose a photograph showing a trench in as much detail as possible (trench board, sandbags, bolt hole etc.) and a soldier in uniform. Explain that this is you, and give some details (for example, perhaps that it is 1915, near Albert, France). These are some examples of questions students might ask, and answers you could give, though how the activity develops is completely up to you and your students.

- *How old are you?*
  I'm 18. I signed up in the autumn of last year. Me and my mates were so keen to serve our country, we went down to enlist together. You don't have to show evidence of your age, and I told them I was 18 then, though my birthday was just this spring.

- *What do you eat?*
  On front-line duty it is mostly tinned bread or biscuits. It is the same every day, and everything has to be kept in tins or the rats get it. We look forward to our time behind lines when the food is better. After about four days in the frontline trenches (more during heavy fighting periods), then maybe a week in support and reserve, we get time behind the lines. Then you get stews, sometimes cheese. The water we get in the trenches is carried from behind the lines and tastes foul – they use chlorine to kill the germs.

- *Do you fight every day?*
  No. As I said before, there is time behind lines and in reserve. When you're on the frontline, mostly the time is pretty dull. Some of the time you are on sentry duty, or you bring up supply from behind the lines, or work on the trench, fixing the boards and so on, or clean your weapons and equipment. When the fighting does happen, then it is very different and frightening, but mostly it is very tedious.

- *What weapons do you have?*
  I have a bolt-action rifle. It can fire 15 rounds per minute. We clean our rifles regularly because if they get jammed it can cost you your life. We have machine guns mounted in the trench. It takes four to six men to work them and they have the fire power of 100 guns. They are nothing against the weapon we have heard the Germans are now using – a gas they fire over the trenches that burns your lungs.

Peer questioning

Ask students to prepare questions to test the knowledge of their peers. This works well as an alternative when you might otherwise have posed the questions yourself or carried out a short quiz or test. Through peer questioning, students revise the topic while writing the questions, and are then tested by their peers' questions. In addition to this double revision, students often feel positive about having the responsibility and control of question setting.

Give students a time limit to write, say, three questions at the back of their books. They can use their notes or textbook at this point. They must know the answer, but must not write it down (or should write it down on another piece of paper). When the time is up, ask students to swap books with the person next to them, and then write the answers to their neighbour's questions. You might give them a couple of minutes to confer with the person next to them about the question (to overcome confusions about spelling and handwriting). After a set time, ask students to swap books back and mark their neighbours' answers.

Variations

- Sometimes it is logistically easier for the whole class to have the same questions – but you can still ask students to suggest the questions. Give them a few minutes to prepare, and then start the quiz, asking students to offer suggestions for the next question as you go along.

- Pre-determine the type of question students can ask. You could limit them to true/false questions, multiple choice, or fuller answer questions. Or give examples of all these options, and encourage students to use a mixture.

- Ask every student to prepare just one question relating to the learning in the current or previous lesson. Ask for a volunteer, or pick a student, to take the 'hot seat' and answer their peer's questions. You could swap the student in the hot seat around – who can answer the most questions correctly?

- Ask a student to pick a peer who they want to answer their question. If the student they pick gets the answer right, it is then their turn to pick one of their peers to answer their question. If they get it wrong, the first student gets to pick another of their class mates to address their question to.

Example

Central government

Subject: Citizenship
Level: Key Stage 3

The following questions were suggested by a Year 8 group at the end of a series of lessons on law making in the UK.

- What am I describing: 'An area of the UK. There are 659 areas like this in the whole country, with an MP from each one'?

- What does MP stand for?

- Can you name the three main political parties in the UK?

- Where do MPs meet to debate and vote on laws?

- What are 'shadow' ministers?

- What are 'back benchers'?

- What is a 'party whip'?

- How many times can the House of Lords pass a bill back to the House of Commons before it becomes a law?

- What does 'devolution' mean?

If this is the answer, what was the question?

Give students the answer to a question: a word, number, or statement. Ask them to take time, on their own or in pairs, to write down what they think the question was.

Variations

- If the answer is very precise, and something they have already come across, this can work as a straightforward test of knowledge.

- Or the answer could be something students have not seen before, and the task is more of a puzzle – they have to think laterally about what the question is.

- Alternatively, give a broad statement that could be the answer to a number of questions, encouraging students to think creatively around the topic. Perhaps the winner could be the most interesting, clever or unusual question, rather than one 'correct' one.

Examples

Gravity and the solar system

Subject: Physics
Level: Key Stage 3

Write the number 164 on the board as students arrive for the lesson. What question do they think this is the answer to? (The number of earth days it takes for Neptune to complete an orbit).

Percentages

Subject: Maths
Level: Key Stage 3

Give students the answer 42, with a bonus mark for including the words 'per cent' in the question. Questions might include: What is 40 + 2? What is 14 x 3? What is the square root of 1,764? What is 16.8 per cent of 250?

Le futur proche

Subject: French
Level: Key Stage 4

The answer is 'Je vais laver ma voiture'. Questions could include: 'Qu'est-ce qu'on va faire demain?'; 'Qu'est-ce qu'on va faire le weekend?'; 'Qu'est-ce que vous faites?'.

Any (other) questions?

Asking students what they want to find out can be a good way of cashing in on their existing knowledge and interest in a topic. Having introduced a topic, but before you explain the structure or breakdown of exactly what you will cover, ask students to discuss in pairs, or write down individually, any questions they have. Feed these questions back to the class, and keep a record of them. Ask a student to act as scribe (onto the board, computer or their book) – this frees you up to lead the feedback and gives the class a greater sense of ownership over the questions.

Explain that you will consider these questions in your teaching of the topic, and that you will also refer back to them during the topic or at the end. At the least, make sure you come back to the list of questions at the end of the topic, and ask students to identify which questions have been answered already (even better, get them to give you the answers). For unanswered questions (there are always a few that are a bit obscure) give students time to research, either in class or at home, or set aside teaching time to work through the answers.

Variations

- This activity can work well in conjunction with the 'Everything you know' activity on page 2 in which students write down what they know so far about a topic. Encourage them to reflect on what they know already before exploring what they would like to know.

- Every time a student asks a question in class which does not directly relate to the material you are covering that lesson, or that you do not know the answer to, keep a record of it. Alternatively, ask students to note down the question themselves and put it into a box on your desk. You may answer some of these questions in the course of your teaching, and could set aside a starter or plenary for answering any remaining questions.

Example

Glaciation

Subject: Geography
Level: Key Stage 3

The following questions were posed by a Year 9 class at the start of their unit on glaciation:

- Why do glaciers have cracks in them?

- Why are glaciers so strong?

- How can scientists work out how thick a glacier is?

- How do animals use the glaciers?

- What is the biggest glacier in the world?

- How high is the highest glacier?

- What is the widest glacier in the world?

- How do glaciers change the world?

- How many glaciers are there in the world?

- When will the next ice age be?

- Why is there a lake in Antarctica, and how do they know it is there?

Section 3
Key words

Write your own dictionary definition

Dictionary definitions, as the name suggests, are clear and concise explanations of a key word or term. It is often the case that while students have studied and copied definitions for all the elements of a process or concept, they may find it more difficult to give a clear definition of the idea or process as a whole. Creating a definition can really help students clarify their understanding. Using notes from class, ask students, on their own or in pairs, to create a concise entry which describes the concept they have covered. This activity results in students having a definition in their notes that they really understand and can use in the future.

You can provide students with an example to help them structure the definition, e.g. *Glaciation* – the process of covering part of the earth's surface with glaciers or masses of ice. *glaciated* adj.

Variations

• For added challenge, ask students to include other key words in their definition. For example, 'neurone' and 'signal' in a definition of 'reflex actions'.

• This activity can also work as a more straightforward recall exercise of key term definitions you have already provided. Start the next lesson by asking students to recall the meaning of the word, and format it as a dictionary entry.

• For a fun twist, challenge students to guess, from a number of options, the real dictionary definition of a word. This works well before you have introduced and defined the word or as revision. Write the new key word on the board. Read out or project three or four possible definitions for the word. One is the real definition and the others are definitions for other words, or are made up. It works well to have one quite similar definition, so that students have to think carefully about which is the right one, and one or two silly or amusing definitions. Ask students to vote for the definition they think is the real one. They can then write the definition in their books. You could also ask students to make up the 'wrong' definitions. Give each pair or group of students a different key word and the real definition. Ask them to create two other definitions to try and catch their classmates out. Or plant one student with the 'real' definition, and then ask everyone to make up a 'false' definition for a new word. Pick a few students to read out their definitions, including the student you know will give the 'true' definition. Ask students to vote for which definition they think is the 'real' one.

Examples

Chartists

Subject: History
Level: Key Stage 4

Students may have studied the social setting of the time, and the origins and development of Chartism. However, they may well not have written a single definition for Chartism other than that it was a 'movement'. Ask them to develop this definition, using their notes on the Chartists.

Electromagnetic radiation

Subject: Physics
Lever: Key Stage 4

Students may be able to list and give a use for all the types of electromagnetic radiation, but can they give a definition of the term 'electromagnetic spectrum' of which these types of radiation are a part?

Marketing

Subject: Business Studies
Level: Key Stage 4

At the start of a lesson introducing the concept of market segmentation, put the term 'Market Segments' on the board, and read students the following definitions:

1. The job description of the chief sales strategist at Terry's, makers of the Chocolate Orange™.

2. A term used to refer to the different groups which marketers divide society into.

3. A term used to refer to the phenomenon of stall-clustering by product type found at many open-air markets.

Match the key word with its definition

Give students a number of key words and, separately, their definitions. Give them a time limit in which to match the words and their meanings.

Variations

- Give each pair of students a pack of words and definitions on card, and ask them to physically sort them – great for kinaesthetic learners.

- Display the words and definitions, mixed up, on the board, and ask volunteers to come up and identify and circle a pair.

- Print the key words and definitions on a worksheet and ask students to draw lines connecting the pairs.

- Match key words and definitions as part of a game of 'key word' dominoes (see page 82 for more details).

Examples

Databases

Subject: ICT
Level: Key Stage 4

For a quick, individual starter, distribute a worksheet listing the mismatched key words and definitions below. Students need to draw a line between each key word and its definition. The activity recaps the terms learned in the previous lesson on data, information and knowledge in relation to ICT.

Keywords and their meanings:
Data: A list of instructions for the computer.
Information: Processing information so that it can be used to make decisions, form judgements and make predictions.
Knowledge: A collection of data with context, which provides meaning.

Expert System: A computer program which can make decisions based on a large quantity of inputted information.

Program: Numbers, words or pictures without context.

Database: A program for storing huge amounts of information.

Measures of average

Subject: Maths

Level: Key Stage 3

Below is the template for a set of cards for revising ways to calculate averages. Distribute packs of these twelve cards to each pair of students, ready cut. Ask students to match the key words and their definitions. For those who finish, they can also sort the third card in each set – a card which shows the average being worked out. Can they finish the calculation and work out the answer in each case?

Mean	The difference between the highest and lowest values in a set of numbers	5 7 2 4 7 5 5 3 1 6 5 56 ÷ 11 =
Median	Sum of all the numbers Amount of numbers	5 7 2 4 7 5 5 3 1 6 5 1 2 3 4 5 5 5 5 6 7 7
Mode	The middle number if all the numbers are placed in order	5 7 2 4 7 5 5 3 1 6 5 1 = 1; 2 = 1; 3 = 1; 4 = 1; 5 = 4; 6 = 1; 2 = 7
Range	The value that occurs most often	5 7 2 4 7 5 5 3 1 6 5 7 – 1 =

Key word pelmanism

Adapt this traditional memory game to use with key words and their definitions. Choose five or six relevant to the lesson and create a set of cards for each pair or small group of students, with one card for each key word and another for its definition.

Instruct each group to lay all the cards face down on the table, and mix them up. The first student to go picks any two cards. He or she turns over the cards so that everyone can see, and gives the group a chance to take a good look! Are these two cards a matching key word and definition? If not, he or she turns the two cards face down again, leaving them in the same place, and the next student has a go. Students not only have to know their key words to tell if they have a matching pair, they also need to remember the position of the cards that have already been turned over. When a student finds a pair – a key word and its definition – they win these two cards and get a 'bonus' turn. The winner is the student with the most cards when all the pairs have been matched.

If you have started the lesson with 'Match the key word with its definition' on page 42, in which students match key words and definitions, this is a good way to finish the lesson – you already have the cards.

Variations

- The game is easier if the cards with the key words on are a different shape or colour from those with the definitions – students are then able to pick one of each.

- Interactive whiteboards allow a whole-class version of this activity. Create a whiteboard document with all your selected key words and their definitions scattered randomly. Place stars, circles or other shapes over all the words and their definitions. Again, the game is much easier if the key words are covered by one shape and the definitions by another (or use the same shape but different colours). It is worth 'locking' the words in place so that they do not move when the overlying shape is moved. Pick a student to come up to the board and move two shapes to reveal the key word and definition underneath. Remind the class to look carefully at what the student has uncovered and where they are, and then cover them back up. Repeat. To add a more competitive edge, divide the class into two teams – the winning team is the team that creates the most pairs.

Example

Los colores

Subject: Spanish
Level: Key Stage 3

Create a pack of pelmanism cards for each pair or group of students, using a grid like the one below. Describe the rules of pelmanism, and start the groups playing.

Yellow	Orange	Blue	White
Black	Green	Red	Brown
Amarillo	Anaranjado	Azul	Blanco
Negro	Verde	Rojo	Marrón

Key word anagrams

Mix up the letters of a key word or words and ask students to figure out what the key word is. Then ask them to define it. This works particularly well if you want a short, snappy starter activity to get students thinking before going on to a more complex 'main' activity.

Variations

- Ask a student, among those first to arrive to lesson, to choose a key word from the last lesson and create an anagram for his or her peers to solve.

- Try this anagram engine for creating anagrams: http://wordsmith.org/anagram

- Ask students to predict the topic of today's lesson by solving the anagram.

Examples

Marketing

Subject: Business Studies
Level: Key Stage 4

Ask students to solve the anagram 'Lesion Penguin Quilt' to discover the topic of the lesson.

Answer: Unique Selling Point.

Hormones

Subject: Biology
Level: Key Stage 4

What is the role of the mystery hormone in the body? 'Person Erg Toe'

Answer: Progesterone.

Key word acronyms

Pick a key word. Challenge students to create a phrase, the first letter of each word corresponding to a letter of the key word. The key word becomes an acronym for the phrase. This can be a quick starter or plenary activity which encourages students to think creatively, can help them remember how to spell key words and/or reflect on and demonstrate their understanding of a concept or idea.

Variations

- With younger groups who may have difficulty remembering a key word, turning the word into an acronym can be a fun memory aid. Allow students to use any words in their phrase, not just those connected to the topic. For example, Magnesium might become '**M**any **a** **g**reen **n**ewt **e**ats **s**andwiches **i**n **u**pturned **m**eringues'. You could choose a winner rewarding the funniest or cleverest.

- Tell students that the phrase they create must reflect their understanding of the topic, or tell you something about the key word. This is more of a challenge, but can produce some impressive results which indicate that students have a firm grasp of the material and can think laterally around the topic. For example, tectonics might be '**T**hick **e**arth **c**rust, **t**he **o**ceanic, **n**udged **i**n **c**urrents, **s**ubducted'. It is much harder to create a sentence, like this one, which makes some sense as a whole. An easier option is simply to select words that are relevant to the topic and start with each of the letters of the key word. This way, tectonics might be '**T**ectonics, **E**arthquakes, **C**ontinental, **T**sunami, **O**ceanic, **N**iigata, **I**gneous, **C**onvection'. Either way, at the end of the activity ask students to feed back to the class, explaining how the words they have chosen cast light on the key word or topic.

- A key word acrostic can be a longer version of this activity in terms of word count, but can be easier than an acronym. Students can suggest a full sentence or line of text for each letter of the key word, rather than having to select a single appropriate word. An acrostic is a poem or other form of writing in which the first letter (or in some cases first syllable or word) of each line spells out another message. In this case the message is the key word. Overall, the acrostic should reflect the concept, feature or idea.

Examples

Houses of Parliament

Subject: Citizenship
Level: Key Stage 3

Year 8 students asked to turn 'Parliament' into an acronym came up with, among others, the following two suggestions:

- **P**ick **a** **r**epresentative, **L**ondon **i**ssues **a**rgue, **m**ake **e**ssential **n**ew **t**erms.

- **P**lace **a**ll **r**epresentatives, **l**ords, **i**mproved, **a**ssembled, **M**Ps **e**lected, **n**ational **t**hinking.

Spelling practice in any topic

Subject: English language
Level: Key Stage 3

Give students time in the lesson to look through their homework and identify a word which the teacher has corrected more than once (perhaps 'necessary', or 'because'). To help them remember how to spell this word they find difficult, they could create a mnemonic, for example, '**N**ever **e**at **c**hips, **e**at **s**moked **s**almon **a**nd **r**emain **y**oung', or '**B**irds **e**at **c**heese **a**nd **u**ncle **s**ucks **e**ggs'.

Map skills

Subject: Geography
Level: Key Stage 3

The following acrostic was written by a Year 7 student on the word 'atlas':

An amazing book with lots of information
Tells you about city's and places
Longitude and longitude
A great book for referring to
Satelite Imagery maps

Crosswords

Don Manley, who sets cryptic crossword puzzles for a range of papers, writes that 'Problem solving' is very much the fashion at the moment in the school curriculum' (D. Manley, 2001; *Chambers Crossword Manual*, Edinburgh: Chambers, page xi). He goes on to say that there are 'some real benefits in struggling with a good crossword: mental discipline and an increased vocabulary are two'.

In the classroom context, crosswords can also be a great puzzle for reinforcing the meanings and spellings of key words. They work well in place of a 'test' at the start of a lesson (after a homework revising key word definitions); in pairs as an absorbing starter while you set up equipment or prepare the main activity; or to consolidate learning at the end of a lesson.

Vary the difficulty of the clues to suit the group and the length of time you want the starter or plenary to take. At the most basic, and where you want to reinforce the definitions of the words, give these as the clues. When students are familiar with the definitions, and for a more fun activity, create clues that are less straightforward and more intriguing.

Variations

- While it is easy to write the clues, creating a good crossword 'grid' by hand is more difficult. There are websites that will generate crosswords for you, if you enter the words, clues and other specifications. For example, try www.armoredpenguin.com/crossword. As well as allowing you to create your own crossword, some websites give access to a database of crosswords already generated, which you can use. For example: www.theteacherscorner.net.

- Give students a blank grid, and ask them to create a crossword of a given number of words (say five or eight), chosen from the topic they have been studying. They have to decide how the words will interlock. It works well if they start by writing the answers into the grid in pencil, and then use a strong colour to draw round the finished grid. They can then rub out the answers and number the empty rectangles. They will also need to write and number the clues. When they have finished they can swap with another student and try and solve their crossword.

- For a quick crossword plenary, project a grid onto the board. Start by writing in a key word (perhaps the title of the topic). Ask students to come up to the board and add other words to the grid. The words must relate to the topic, and they must 'cross' the existing words, so each word must share a letter with at least one other word. For example, in a Key Stage 3 Physics lesson you might start with the word 'reflection'. A student might add 'mirror', crossing 'reflection' at the 'o'. Another student might add 'scatter', sharing an 'r' with the first 'r' in 'mirror'. If a word is added in a row or column directly next to an existing word, any new words created by the overlap must make sense too (which is hard to do).

Examples

African music

Subject: Music
Level: Key Stage 4

Clues

Across
2. A Senegalese relative of the African American banjo.
4. A hand-held drum made in Nigeria, West Africa.
5. A Middle-Eastern drum played with the fingers.
6. Also known as a banana bell.
8. A gourd containing seeds that rattle when shaken.

Down
1. A traditional double bell, held in the hand and struck with a stick.
3. A hollow gourd loosely covered in a web of seeds.
5. Also known as the 'healing drum'.
7. A 21-string harp-lute from the Gambia.

Battle of Hastings

Subject: History
Level: Key Stage 3

A Year 7 crossword that reinforces key terms related to the battle and names of key figures.

Clues

Across

4. The Norwegians fought Harold Godwinson at _____ Bridge.
6. Harold was killed at this battle.
8. Harald's surname.

Down

1. Edward the _____.
2. Which of the three men who wanted the throne did **not** think he was promised it by Edward?
3. Where was William from?
5. Knights on horseback.
7. A tapestry of the invasion of England.

Circulatory system

Subject: Physical Education
Level: Key Stage 4

A GCSE PE class was divided into two teams. Points were available for each key word, relating to the circulatory system, which could be added to the grid on the board, crossing existing words. Below is the grid part-way through the activity.

						H						
c	i	r	c	u	l	A	t	o	r	y		
A						E						
P						M						
I						O						
L						G					S	
L					p	L	a	t	e	l	E	T
A						O					P	
R						B					T	
Y						I					U	
						N					M	

Word searches

The basic, well-known idea is to find words (usually connected to a particular theme) in a grid of random-seeming letters. In itself this search-and-highlight exercise does not teach students much. However, if you add an extra step, this activity can help students learn the definitions of key words. Instead of simply listing all the words hidden in the grid on the next page, list the definitions or clues. Students must first identify the key word they are looking for, and then find it.

Variations

• There are many websites which will let you create a word search to your specifications, including your selected key words, e.g. www.teachers-direct.co.uk/resources/ wordsearches. In addition to creating a printed version, this website also creates an 'interactive' version, allowing students to identify words on screen.

Examples

Population

Subject: Geography
Level: Key Stage 4

Clues
1. The number of births per 1,000 people in the population, per year.
2. A term used to describe a situation when there are too many people living in an area relative to the number of resources.
3. Movement of people.
4. Birth rate – death rate.
5. The number of children who die before their first birthday, per 1,000 live births in the population.
6. Movement of people into a country or area.
7. The average number of years a person is expected to live.
8. A rapid increase in the population size of a country or area.
9. A term used to describe the perfect balance between the number of people living in a given area and the resources of that area.
10. The number of deaths per 1,000 people in the population, per year.
11. (Birth rate + immigration) – (death rate + emigration).
12. Movement of people out of a country or area.
13. A term used to describe a situation when there are too few people living in an area to be able to fully exploit the resources of the area.

e	t	a	r	h	t	r	i	b	e	n	u	a	r	a	n	i	p	e	e	r
g	x	a	t	n	p	a	m	a	a	p	e	c	e	t	g	c	e	t	t	a
n	a	u	m	n	t	c	i	i	n	I	s	s	t	a	r	i	a	a	t	l
a	g	u	l	n	n	a	i	e	x	t	d	u	r	t	f	r	n	a	o	n
h	t	a	l	o	i	g	m	r	p	a	e	e	h	t	y	o	t	a	l	n
c	r	a	r	o	v	e	r	p	o	p	u	l	a	t	i	o	n	m	m	i
n	o	i	t	a	l	u	p	o	p	m	u	m	i	t	p	o	o	i	m	i
o	a	a	e	r	n	a	i	t	t	l	a	l	a	p	h	o	i	g	n	i
i	l	t	p	p	a	m	v	e	t	o	a	r	o	n	l	r	t	r	t	r
t	g	p	u	x	p	x	u	o	p	t	g	i	u	p	r	o	a	a	i	a
a	i	a	e	r	u	t	t	i	r	l	a	m	l	t	e	r	l	t	e	c
l	a	l	l	e	a	m	i	o	m	g	e	t	t	l	n	e	u	i	e	c
u	t	p	I	p	n	l	m	m	u	e	r	n	p	a	n	t	p	o	e	d
p	o	p	u	l	a	t	i	o	n	e	x	p	l	o	s	i	o	n	i	l
o	t	a	f	t	n	c	a	n	h	a	i	t	h	o	n	o	p	v	l	p
p	u	o	l	a	n	r	y	l	c	t	u	o	m	i	g	n	r	e	t	p
l	t	t	f	p	c	t	a	i	f	r	e	t	e	g	l	a	e	o	f	n
a	i	n	o	i	t	a	r	g	i	m	e	a	y	l	a	h	d	e	n	n
u	i	l	I	f	e	e	x	p	e	c	t	a	n	c	y	n	n	o	i	c
t	r	a	t	e	y	p	p	l	b	l	r	n	s	t	n	u	u	i	a	g
c	g	a	a	n	n	n	i	c	t	t	u	g	i	e	o	t	g	n	a	a
a	t	i	l	t	t	a	e	p	o	m	t	a	l	u	i	t	m	t	l	m

Make a sentence with this word

Write a key word up on the board. Ask students, on their own or in pairs, to create a sentence using that word. The sentence can be anything they want, but must demonstrate the, or a, meaning of the word.

This is a great starter for introducing new terms, particularly those that are used in day-to-day language but have different subject-specific meanings, or those that have multiple meanings. Suggesting a sentence can make a change and be more fun than simply giving a definition. The activity encourages students to consider their existing understanding of the word, before building a subject specific meaning.

Variations

- This activity can also be used as a plenary, with key words that have been learned during the lesson. Ask students to shut their books, and write a key word or term on the board. As before, students have to create a sentence, including the word, which explains the meaning of the word. Bonus points for those sentences that are the funniest or most creative, while still conveying the meaning of the word.

Examples

Map skills

Subject: Geography
Level: Key Stage 3

Geography students developing their map skills learn about contour lines, which give information about the 'relief' of the landscape. Before introducing the topic, ask students to write a sentence including the word 'relief' to get responses such as: 'I gave money to Comic Relief'; 'What a relief, Geography was over'; 'It is a relief that I could answer the questions in the test'. Having unpicked what these sentences tell us about the meaning of the word, introduce students to the way it is used in Geography: relief as the highs and lows of landscape rather than emotion.

Methods of production

Subject: Business Studies
Level: Key Stage 4

After a lesson studying methods of production, ask GCSE Business Studies students to create a sentence including the term 'capital intensive'. Responses might include 'The new technology for the production line was very capital intensive'; or 'Sam's new interest in deep sea diving was very capital intensive'.

What key word am I?

This is a version of the party game where each guest has the name of a celebrity stuck to their forehead. You have to go around asking other guests questions to try and figure out your identity.

Give each student a sticky note or label. Ask them to choose a key word from a list or topic and write it onto the sticky label. Next, they should stick the label on their partner's forehead, without showing him or her the word.

Taking it in turns, students have to ask questions to try and work out what their key term is. Their partner can only answer 'Yes' or 'No'. They should keep a record of how many questions they ask – the winner is the person who works out their word using the fewest number of questions.

Talk to students first about the best questioning strategy and what kind of questions might help them narrow down the field – going straight to 'Am I x?' is not the most efficient approach!

Variations

- Give each pair of students a pack of around ten cards, each with a key word on it. One student looks at the first card, the other student asks questions (to which the answers can only be 'Yes' or 'No') to help guess what the word is. When the guesser gets it right, he or she starts asking questions about the next word in the pack. How many can he or she guess correctly in a limited time? If there are enough cards left, the pair can swap roles.

- Choose a key word, and select one student to take the 'hot seat' at the front of the class. They must try and guess their word, addressing their questions to different students of their choice.

Examples

Periodic table

Subject: Chemistry
Level: Key Stage 3

Write the elements of the periodic table on sticky labels and distribute them, one to each student. They must not look at their element but stick it straight on their forehead (or, perhaps easier, ask each student to stick their sticker on their partner's forehead). Give each pair a copy of the periodic table and help students think about questions they might ask to work out which element they are. They could start by asking: 'Am I a metal or a non-metal?'; 'Am I in an even- or an odd- numbered group?'; 'Do I have similar properties to chlorine (i.e. Am I in the same group)?'; 'Am I in a period that has lots of elements in it?' Then they could start narrowing down: 'Am I in group number 7?'; 'Am I near to magnesium?'

Glaciation

Subject: Geography
Level: Key Stage 3

Ask students to pick one of the following terms for their partner. They must write down the term, without showing their partner (though they do not need to stick it on their partner's forehead, they can simply keep it hidden):

- Cirque.

- Kettle Hole.

- Arête.

- Horn.

- U-shaped valley.

- Hanging valley.

- Striation.

- Esker.

- Drumlin.

- Erratic.

To guess their feature, students might start with questions like: 'Am I a feature created by erosion?'; 'Am I created by one or more cirque glaciers?'; 'Am I a small feature?'

Section 4

Game show

Bingo

Ask students to draw a 'bingo grid': four, six, or eight squares, depending on the length of time and number of key words you have. Project or write a list of key words on the board, and ask students to pick enough words to fill their grid: one word in each square. Remind them that they should pick words that they know the meaning of.

The teacher then selects these words, one at a time, and if a word in their grid is picked, students cross it out. The difference from regular Bingo is that, instead of saying the word itself, you read out a definition of the word. This means that students need to know the meaning of their words to be able to cross them off. It also means that they get to hear good definitions for these words: once as you play, and once at the end as you go through the answers.

The winner (who shouts out 'Bingo') is the first to get a line or 'full house', depending on the time you have available.

Variations

• Mini-whiteboards work well for creating a quick grid.

• Use questions where the answers are the key words, instead of simply reading the definitions.

• A version of Bingo, popular in the field of development education, is known as Globingo. In this case each 'square' in the grid contains an action or a question. Rather than answering the question yourself, the idea is to find someone in the room who has completed the action or knows (or can make a good estimate of) the answer to the question. Having found someone, get them to write their answer into the box and sign it. The aim is to get a different person to put their signature in each of the 'boxes' (you cannot sign any yourself, and you can't get another student to sign more than one box). The winner is the first person to have every box signed. The activity works well to get students moving around the room, talking to other students. The feedback is the crucial part of the activity in terms of development of understanding: Who gave an answer for question two? What did you write? Why? Anyone got any other answers?

Examples

Elements of music

Subject: Music
Level: Key Stage 4

Below is one student's half-finished Bingo grid for a music lesson on the elements of music, and the definitions that have been read so far:

Clue 1: The distance between two notes.
Clue 2: Heavy use of sharps, flats and naturals.
Clue 3: A musical 'sentence'.
Clue 4: The other name for this contains the word 'surprise'. It sounds as though the music is coming to an end, but then you get a minor chord.
Clue 5: The word used to describe a repeated pattern of notes in classical music.
Clue 6: A musical device when one instrument or voice plays a tune that has just been played by another.

One student's 'elements of music' Bingo grid:

Riff	Key signature	Imperfect cadence
Chromatism	Tempo	Tonality

Mental maths

Subject: Maths
Level: Key Stage 4

Bingo can work as a form of mental maths test. Students will need to complete each calculation to know if they have the answer. The first few questions in this game of Bingo might be:

Clue 1: 5 per cent of 300.
Clue 2: 30 ÷ 6.
Clue 3: The square root of 64.
Clue 4: 2 – 1.62.

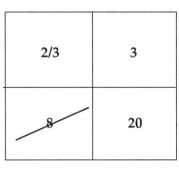

Global citizenship

Subject: Citizenship
Level: Key Stage 4

The Globingo worksheet below, which introduces issues related to the global dimension of Citizenship, is adapted from a resource by Stephen Fairbrass, available at the Just Business website. You can find the original version, and the answers, at www.jusbiz.org, a website which provides information and activities about global and ethical issues for students and teachers of Business Studies, Economics and Citizenship.

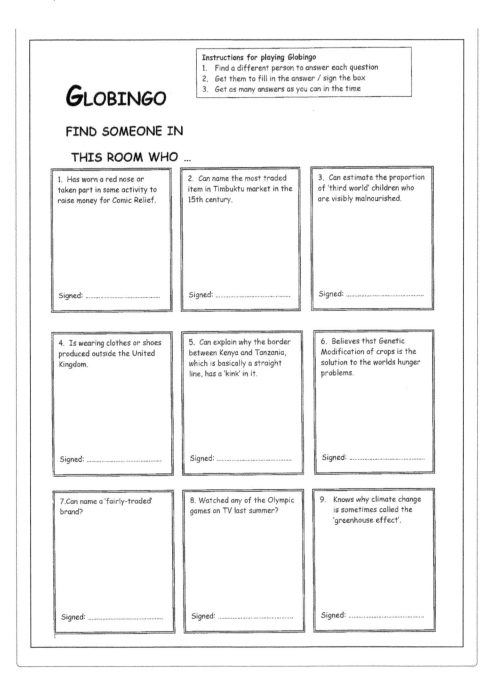

GLOBINGO

Instructions for playing Globingo
1. Find a different person to answer each question
2. Get them to fill in the answer / sign the box
3. Get as many answers as you can in the time

FIND SOMEONE IN

THIS ROOM WHO ...

1. Has worn a red nose or taken part in some activity to raise money for Comic Relief. Signed:	2. Can name the most traded item in Timbuktu market in the 15th century. Signed:	3. Can estimate the proportion of 'third world' children who are visibly malnourished. Signed: ....
4. Is wearing clothes or shoes produced outside the United Kingdom. Signed:	5. Can explain why the border between Kenya and Tanzania, which is basically a straight line, has a 'kink' in it. Signed:	6. Believes that Genetic Modification of crops is the solution to the worlds hunger problems. Signed: ....
7. Can name a 'fairly-traded' brand? Signed:	8. Watched any of the Olympic games on TV last summer? Signed:	9. Knows why climate change is sometimes called the 'greenhouse effect'. Signed: ....

Just a minute

As on the Radio 4 show of the same name, students must attempt to talk for one minute on a topic you have selected for them. Of course, they must do so without hesitation, repetition or deviation!

This is a good game for revision at the end of a topic, or to consolidate an idea or process covered in a previous lesson. You can ask for volunteers to talk for a minute on the topic, or pick two or three students at random, having given the class time to revise and prepare.

Pick three different students as judges – one to watch for hesitation, one for repetition and one for deviation. Give them whistles or 'hooters' or ask them to put up their hand when they hear the competitor 'trip up'. Hesitations are easier to spot, but you may need to act as a final arbiter on repetitions and deviations. A fourth student could be in charge of keeping a record of the time, or use an internet countdown (see page xiv). In either case you will need to stop the timer as soon as one of the judges 'hoots' or puts their hand up, but restart if the halt was unfounded.

The winner is generally the first student to get to a minute, or more likely the student that gets the furthest towards a minute!

Variations

• This activity also works well in pairs. One student times and listens out for hesitations, repetitions and deviations. The other talks for as long as possible without hesitating, repeating or deviating! This variation involves students who would otherwise be uncomfortable about carrying out the challenge in front of the whole class, and can act as a 'practice round' for the activity above.

Examples

Various

Subject: Design and Technology
Level: Key Stage 4

'Just a minute' topics for GCSE Design and Technology might include 'resistant materials', 'textiles', or 'food composition'.

Various

Subject: English Literature
Level: Key Stage 4

In English lessons students could be challenged to talk about their text or author, whether that is Shakespeare or Carol Ann Duffy.

Who Wants to be a Millionaire?™

Students enjoy the familiar format of this well-known television show, based on multiple choice questions. You can adapt it to suit your topic and group. This is a longer starter or plenary activity, and takes a while to prepare.

You will need to write 12 questions, each with four possible answers. The questions should be increasingly difficult, and you may want to include some joke options in earlier questions. You can either read the questions out to the class, or prepare a computer version you can project.

Ask all students, working on their own, to write down the letter that corresponds to the answer they think is right (A, B, C or D). In the television show there is no time limit, but you will need either to set one, or give students a warning when they need to have written their answer down.

After each question, give the answer. All students who got the first answer right 'win' £500. For each subsequent question students get right, the winning total goes up (£1,000, £2,000, £5,000, £10,000, £20,000, £50,000, £75,000, £150,000, £250,000, £500,000 and finally £1 million). You will have to rely on students' honesty as to whether they got the answer right. You might want to ask all those still 'in' to raise their hand after each round, but encourage those who are 'out' to carry on writing their answers. If students get the £1,000 question right, then even if they get a subsequent question wrong, they still win £1,000. If they get up to £50,000, then they keep this sum even if they get one of the next few questions wrong.

In the television version, contestants have three lifelines that they can use if they are not sure of the answer: '50:50' (where two of the multiple choice options are removed), 'Phone a friend' (when they can ask a friend the answer), and 'Ask the audience'. After a difficult question, you could ask students who want a lifeline to raise their hands. If more than half the class want a lifeline then ask students to vote on which one they would like to use. Because the whole class is playing you could adapt the options to: '50:50', 'Ask the teacher', and 'Ask the class'. For the last of these options, ask students to raise their hand to indicate which of the four answers they think is correct – so that everyone can see everyone else's answer. Students can only use each lifeline once – you could write the lifelines onto the board and rub them off as they are used.

Variations

- Instead of getting the whole class involved, pick a single contestant. Ask them to nominate a 'friend' beforehand in case they want to 'Phone a friend'. You can act as compère, or pick a student for this role. Use of the catch-phrase 'Is that your final answer?' causes amusement.

- Another lifeline could be 'Pass' – you will need to prepare spare questions in case this option is selected.

- There are templates available on the internet (search 'Who Wants to be a Millionaire template schools'), which you can adapt for your topic and class. Some include sound effects.

- You can find the theme tune on YouTube!

Examples

The Weimar Republic

Subject: History
Level: Key Stage 4

Questions from a Who Wants to be a Millionaire?™ quiz used in History to revise 'The Weimar Republic'.

£500 question:
What was the name of the German town in which a new government was set up in February 1919?
A: Wiemar B: Warsaw C: Weimar D: Watford

£1,000 question:
What was the name of the elected parliament in the new republic?
A: Reichstag B: Parliament C: House of Representatives D: House of Commons

£2,000 question:
What number was the article which said that, in an emergency, the president could pass decrees without the Reichstag?
A: 12 B: 42 C: 48 D: 58

£5,000 question:
What was the name of the March 1920 rebellion which aimed to bring back the Kasier?
A: Kapp Punch B: Kape Putsch C: Knap Putsch D: Kapp Putsch

£10,000 question:

What did the German government fail to pay to the French that led to the invasion of the Ruhr?

A: Taxes B: Reparations C: Inflation D: Steel

£20,000 question:

The Spartacist uprising in January 1919 was led by Rosa Luxemburg and ... ?

A: Karl Leibknecht B: Karl Leibher C: Hans Leibknecht D: Hans Leibher

£50,000 question:

What is the party name 'Nazi' short for?

A: Nazi Party B: The National Aryan Party C: National Socialists D: Autarky

£75,000 question:

What is the English translation of the title of the book *Mein Kampf* which Hitler wrote while in prison for his involvement in the failed Munich Putsch?

A: My life B: My country C: My beliefs D: My struggle

£150,000 question:

What year was the Munich Putsch?

A: 1922 B: 1923 C: 1924 D: 1925

£250,000 question:

What was the profession of Paul Klee, one of the leaders of German cultural flowering during the 1920s?

A: An architect B: An artist C: A singer D: A writer

£500,000 question:

How many seats in the Reichstag did the Nazi Party have in July 1932 – they were then the largest party?

A: 30 B: 130 C: 230 D: 330

£1 million question:

When did Hitler declare himself absolute ruler of Germany, using Article 48?

A: December 1932 B: January 1933 C: February 1933 D: March 1933

Answers: C; A; C; D; B; A; C; D; B; B; C; B

Pictionary™

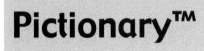

Another fun way of reinforcing the meaning of key words. Ask for a volunteer, or pick a student. Give them a card with a key word written on it, and a board pen. Give the student 30 seconds in which to think about how they might picture the word, and then ask them to start drawing. The aim of the rest of the class is to guess what is being drawn, without the aid of gesticulation from the 'draw-er'. Take answers from students who put up their hands, or allow students to shout out. The 'draw-er' stops drawing when the word is guessed or, if you set a timer going, when the allotted time runs out.

Ask the student who guesses correctly to say what it is about the picture that reflects the key word for them. Can they also give a definition of the key word? You can repeat the process once or twice more, picking different students and different key words, depending on the amount of time you have available.

Variations

- You can make this quick activity into a longer team game. You will need to divide the class into two teams, and have more key word cards prepared. Pick a team to start, and ask them to volunteer (or you can select) a 'draw-er' from within the team. Use a timer (a minute works well) and ask the 'draw-er' to draw their word within that time. Only their own team can guess the word, and if they get the right word within the time, they get a point for their team. If the opposite team shout out the word, the point still goes to the drawing team. Repeat the process for the other team. Allow two or three rounds and see who scores the highest.

- Give the 'draw-er' a longer time limit, say three minutes, and a pack of several cards. How many can they get the class, or their team, to guess within the time limit? They may 'pass' on one word, but otherwise they must work their way through the cards in order.

Examples

The spread of microbes

Subject: Biology
Level: Key Stage 3

At the end of a lesson on the spread of microbes, or at the start of the next lesson, ask students to draw the ways in which microbes can be transmitted. You might give the first student the word 'animals', another 'touch', and another 'water'. Explain to the rest of the class that they are guessing the type of transmission from the drawing. Ask the student who guesses correctly to explain a bit more about the type of transmission – for example, for 'animals' they might say that some animals carry harmful microbes that are passed on to a person if they are scratched or bitten by that animal. Can the student give an example, e.g. mosquitoes carry malaria?

Verb revision

Subject: Spanish
Level: Key Stage 3

Give the first student to arrive in class a card with a Spanish verb written on it (perhaps 'Beber' or 'Mirar') and a board pen. Ask the student to draw a picture of someone doing the action that the word describes, for the rest of the class to guess, in Spanish, as they arrive. Once a student guesses correctly, ask them to give the English translation to reinforce their understanding (in this case 'to drink' and 'to look at').

Rapidough™

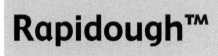

This starter or plenary works in a similar way to Pictionary™, but with modelling from clay instead of drawing. You will need some play dough or modelling clay for this game, which is based on the board game of the same name.

Pick a student and a key word, and give them a set time in which to model the object the word describes. The rest of the class (or team if you divide the class into teams) must guess the word without verbal clues or gesticulations!

This only works well with the names of physical objects; modelling processes such as 'digestion', or ideas such as 'facism' are tough!

Variations

- Add an extra level of complexity. The students guessing the answer must give the name of the object, and you could also ask them to provide other relevant information, such as the reason it has been selected for modelling, or the category it fits into. For example, Key Stage 3 Biology students studying classification could guess the organism being modelled, and give the kingdom, phylum and even class and order that it is part of.

- If the key words you want to cover in the starter or plenary are too tricky to model, try giving the 'model-er' the name of an easier-to-model object related to the key word. The students guessing have to identify the object being modelled, and then the term the object is a clue to. For example, Key Stage 3 Geography students studying the weather may look at how weather affects our lives. Pick students to model a tractor, a football and a lorry. From these, the rest of the class must guess the professions they represent. Why are these professions particularly susceptible to changes in the weather?

Examples

Noun revision

Subject: French
Level: Key Stage 3

This activity works well in language lessons – but, in this case, students must provide the word for the modelled e.g. cat, tree, car, bus, in French.

Introduction to the Laboratory

Subject: Chemistry
Level: Key Stage 3

Ask Year 7 students to model different items of laboratory equipment, and the guessing students give their proper names. For example: measuring cylinder; pipette; tripod; test tube; thermometer; spatula.

Blockbusters

Blockbusters began showing on British TV in 1983. It was a trivia show in which contestants had to answer questions correctly to move across or down a board made up of 20 hexagons with letters in them. Questions followed the style: 'What R is a form of precipitation?'

Blockbusters can be easily adapted for the classroom: you just need a grid, 20 key words, and two teams. Take the first letter of each key word and place them in the hexagons. These should preferably be all different letters, but there can be repeats if necessary. Create a question for each letter, the answer to which is the key word. It is worth bearing in mind that occasionally, if neither team gets the answer, you may need an additional backup question, for which the answer is either the same key word or a different key word with the same first letter.

Pick the first letter, and ask the question for this letter. Both teams can answer the question. You can either look for the fastest hand up in either team, or choose two students from each team (a different two for each question), and take the fastest hand up between the two (or fastest 'beep' if you have 'hooters'). If the student you select gets the right answer, that hexagon on the grid is shaded in with the team colour. They get to pick the next letter too (perhaps using the catchphrase, 'Can I have an N, please Bob!'). If the first team to give an answer gets it wrong, the question is passed to the other team. If they still do not get it right, you use a backup question for the same hexagon, which either team can answer.

The aim of one team is to get a line of shaded hexagons down the board. The connection can be made in any way, as long as the hexagons are touching. The other team must make the connection across the board. The winning team is the first to get that connection. See 'Variations' section for ideas on which team goes across and which down.

Variations

- In the original game show a team of two children competed against a single child. The child on his or her own had to work down the board, having one fewer space to get across than the pair. You can either split the class unevenly to replicate this, or, if you have time for more than one game, alternate the direction between equally sized teams. Another way to allocate the direction is to ask a starter question, and give the shorter direction to the team that answer quickest/correctly. Alternatively, remove the last column, so that each team has only four hexagons to win.

- The 'Teachers-direct' website allows your to create your own 'quiz-busters' quiz along the Blockbusters format, producing a game for an interactive whiteboard to your specifications. It also has a directory of quizzes already created by teachers, and ready to use: www.teachers-direct.co.uk/resources/quiz-busters.

- You can find the Blockbusters theme tune on YouTube!

Examples

Rivers

Subject: Geography
Level: Key Stage 3

Below is a possible grid for 'Rivers' Blockbusters in Geography. Here are the clues that have played so far in this half-finished game:

Which 'W' describes a ridge of land that separates two river systems?
Which 'S' is a form of transportation by a river, in which stones are 'bounced' along the river bed?
Which 'C' is the term for the point where two rivers meet?
Which 'U' is the term for the first part of the river course, close to the source?
Which 'A' is the term for a form of erosion in which small stones 'sandpaper' the river bed?
Which 'R' describes a stretch of quickly moving water in the upper course of a river?
Which 'O' is the name of a U-shaped lake which forms from a meander?

Halfway through a game of 'Rivers' Blockbusters:

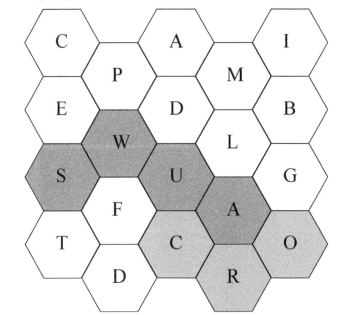

Taboo™

This activity is based on the board game of the same name, in which contestants must describe a word but without saying a number of 'taboo' words.

You will need to prepare several cards, each with a key word at the top, and some 'taboo' words underneath. You need to strike a balance of making some obvious words forbidden, but leaving some scope to describe the key word! Make two copies of each card.

Pick a student, or if you have divided the class into teams, ask one of the teams to put forward a contestant. Give one of the cards to this student, and give them a moment to read it through and ask you any questions. Give the other copy of the card to a 'censor', a neutral student or a student from the opposite team. Equip the censor with a whistle or 'hooter'. This student should sound the 'hooter' if the contestant says any of the taboo words, any part of these words, or any part of the key word.

Remind the contestant that gestures and sounds are not allowed – only words – and that they have a set time to get the class, or their team mates, to guess the key word they are describing.

Variations

- In the board game itself, contestants are given several cards, and their team mates must correctly guess as many as possible in a given time. This variation can work well at the end of topic when you have a number of key words.

- Switch the roles of 'guesser' and 'explainer'. You would normally have one student trying to explain the word, and the rest of their team or class guessing. Instead, sit a student in front of the board, but with their back to it, facing the rest of the class. Write a key word onto the board. Challenge the rest of the class to get the student in the 'hot seat' to say the word on the board: they can use synonyms, put the word into context, use definitions, but may not say the word itself. You could split the class into two teams, with a 'hot seat' for each team. Both teams try to explain the word to their team member – whichever team's 'hot seat' gets it first, wins a point. This can be a noisy activity – you may want to limit the number of students in each team who can do the explaining. Instead of writing on the board, use a computer and projector to project the word. This way, if you create a series of slides with different words, you can easily scroll through the words as they are guessed. How many words can the student in the 'hot seat' guess in a given time?

Examples

Shape

Subject: Maths
Level: Key Stage 3

Taboo™ cards for a Maths class learning about construction and locus might look like this:

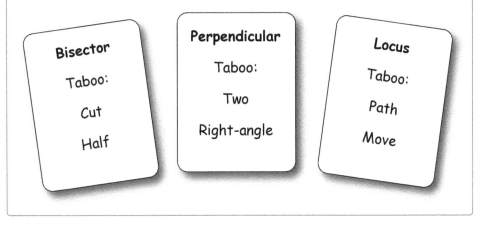

Bisector

Taboo:

Cut

Half

Perpendicular

Taboo:

Two

Right-angle

Locus

Taboo:

Path

Move

Coasts

Subject: Geography
Level: Key Stage 3

Below are some ideas for Taboo™ cards from a Year 8 Geography lesson.

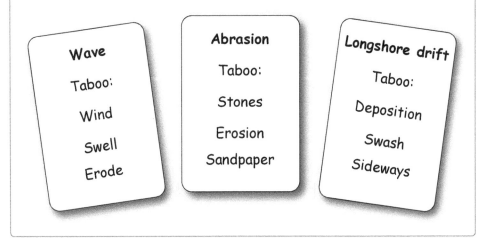

Wave

Taboo:

Wind

Swell

Erode

Abrasion

Taboo:

Stones

Erosion

Sandpaper

Longshore drift

Taboo:

Deposition

Swash

Sideways

Mallett's Mallet

Adapted from Timmy Mallet's game from the *Wacaday* show (but without the mallet), this is a word association activity. It is a fun game which relies on students having key words on the tip of their tongue!

Pick two students, and award them ten starting points each. Pick a topic, usually one you have been covering in class, and write this on the board. Finally, pick a key word – it works well if this is central to the topic, perhaps 'Volcano' if the topic is 'Plate Tectonics'. Choose one student to start, who must say an associated word. The second student must say a word associated to the word the first student says, and so on. The rules are that students must not hesitate or repeat, and need to stay on topic.

Each time a student hesitates or repeats or, in your opinion (or that of an appointed student judge) goes off-topic, they loose a point. You then restart with another key word (say, 'Earthquake', following the example above). The winner is the person to retain the most points in a given time.

Variations

- A whole-class variation of this game is word association tennis. Divide the class into two teams, and, as above, pick a topic. Choose a student from one of the teams to 'serve': they say a key word from the topic. The idea is to 'hit' the word association 'ball' back and forth between the teams. You can either encourage students to self-select who will return the 'ball', by shouting out a word, or putting up their hand. An alternative approach is to give all the students in each team a go in a predetermined pattern, so that each student knows when it is their turn to 'return' the ball. If the 'ball' is dropped (a hesitation or repetition, or going 'off-topic', which you or a student referee call), then the opposite team wins a point (15: love), and they 'serve' for the next point, with another key word.

- An easier version is that the word must be associated with the original key word or the 'topic', rather than with the last word that is said. This gives the students more scope and a little bit longer to prepare their word!

Examples

Hardware

Subject: ICT
Level: Key Stage 4

A point in 'ICT Mallet's Mallet', or a rally in 'ICT Tennis' might run something like this:

Starting word/serve: Input device
Student/team 1: Manual
Student/team 2: Keyboard
Student/team 1: Touch screen
Student/team 2: Visual display unit
Student/team 1: Monitor...

Introduction to Geography

Subject: Geography
Level: Key Stage 3

A 'Types of Geography' word association round, with association to the topic rather than the last word, might run like this:

Topic: Physical Geography
Student/team 1: Volcanoes
Student/team 2: Lakes
Student/team 1: Rivers
Student/team 2: Weather
Student/team 1: Rocks
Student/team 2: Coasts...

Dominoes

Students are generally familiar with dominoes: the sets of rectangular tiles with one face divided by a line into two squares, each marked with a number of spots. A common game to play with dominoes involves players setting down a domino in turn, matching the number on one side of their tile to the same number on one of the tiles already on the table.

A similar game can be played with key words and definitions: key word dominoes. It takes some preparation: each pair or group of students will need a set of key word dominoes. Credit-card-sized pieces of card work well, with a line drawn vertically down the middle. On one end print a key word and on the other a definition (but not the one that matches it). For the game to work well, you need several key words and definitions, or a double set with each word appearing twice but in combination with a different definition.

Each student is dealt the same number of 'definition dominoes' (say five or six). The pair should decide between them who will lay a tile first: they could roll a dice, or you could pick all students on the left of each pair. When it is their turn, students try to lay a tile, matching one end (either a word or definition) to the matching definition or word already on the table.

If a student cannot go, they pass, and should pick up an extra 'definition domino' from the un-dealt pile. The game is over when one student has put down all their tiles (they are the winner) or when the game is blocked and neither student can go even though they have passed and 'picked up' until the un-dealt pile is finished. The winner in this case is the student who has put down the most 'definition dominoes'.

Variations

- For a shorter starter or plenary, ask students to work in pairs to put together a line of key word dominoes from their pack of domino cards, with definitions always touching the key word they describe.

- Distribute a key word domino card to every student in the class. Pick a student to start, who reads out the key word on their domino. All the other students look at their card, and the student who has the definition puts up their hand, and reads out the definition. They then read the key word on the other side of the domino, and again, everybody checks again to see if they have the definition. Repeat until every key word and definition is matched.

- Rather than matching key words and definitions, students can match pairs of key words. This version of the dominoes game is less rigid: the term or phrase in the face of a domino card could match more than one other phrase or word, and therefore more than one tile. Students have to use their understanding of a topic to look for a possible match among their dominoes, and then justify the choice they have made to their partner or the rest of the group.

Examples

Sikhism

Subject: Religious Education
Level: Key Stage 3

Distribute a set of domino cards, created from the template below, to each pair. Ask them to create a line of dominoes cards, matching each key word to its definition.

Kanga	Sikh scripture

Kara	Uncut hair

Guru Granth Sahib	Steel bracelet

Kesh	Sikh place of worship

Gurdwara	Cotton underwear

Kaccha	Steel swords

Kirpan	Community of Sikh men and women

Khalsa	Wooden comb

Plate tectonics

Subject: Geography
Level: Key Stage 3

Provide each pair or group of students with a set of cards like those below, and start them playing dominoes. They must try to create pairs of words that are linked in some way. If they can convince the rest of the group that there is a geographical link between two words, then the match is allowed and they can lay their card.

You could give some examples of explanations, such as:

• Tectonic plate and convection current are linked because tectonic plates are moved around by convection currents in the mantle.

• Fold mountains and constructive plate boundary are linked because fold mountains form at constructive plate boundaries as the continental plate is forced up.

• Subduction zone and oceanic plate are linked because the oceanic plate is forced under the continental plate in the subduction zone at destructive plate boundaries.

You may be called upon to arbitrate where students can't agree whether or not an explanation for a match is sufficiently convincing! The blank dominoes are 'any word' cards. A student can lay it and say a key word of their choice, as long as it is related to the topic. It should not be a word that has already been put down. Again, as long as they can convince their group that the word they have said is linked to the word they are laying it next to, they can go ahead.

Fold mountains	Constructive plate boundary

Convection currents	Richter scale

Epicentre	Oceanic plate

Destructive plate boundary	Focus

Collision plate boundary	Continental plate			Volcano

	Convection current		Tectonic plate	Magma

Crust	Earthquakes		Subduction zone	Lava

Section 5

Figure it out

Mystery object

Present students with an object. Ask them to think about, or discuss in pairs, the significance of this item in light of what they have been learning. What do they think the object is? Why? How is it linked to the topic they have been studying?

Students respond well to the 'mystery' element of this activity and it can really get them thinking.

Depending on how 'mysterious' the item is, students may not get the right answer. You can help them through your feedback to their guesses, steering subsequent guesses and getting students thinking: 'That's possible, but it's not really related to the Cold War', or 'Could be, but think a bit more about the shape of the object'.

When the allotted time is up, or you feel students' engagement is waning, let them know the answer. Or you can offer a small reward to any team that can tell you next lesson.

Variations

- Instead of a mystery object, use a mystery image (a photograph or picture), a mystery number, or even a mystery sound. Depending on the mystery image, you could ask students to guess what it is, where it is, or what is happening/has happened.

- Rather than asking students to focus on guessing what the object is, ask them to give any observations they have about the object, to help build up a picture of what it is for, e.g. 'It is very light', 'It has no markings on the surface'.

- What five questions do students think, if answered, would give them enough information to work out what the object is? Questions which start with the following words can be helpful – students could ask one of each. Who? What? Why? Where? When?

- If you do not have a suitable mystery item to hand, an alternative is to provide students clues to help them guess the mystery person, event, or even process you have in mind. Start with broad clues ('The person I am thinking of was a significant figure in post-war politics') and slowly narrow down ('This person was not present at the conference at Yalta, but was present at Potsdam'; 'This person had a doctrine that the US would support countries fighting against communism').

Examples

African music

Subject: Music
Level: Key Stage 4

Having learned about African musical instruments, show GCSE Music students a picture of an instrument they have not studied, or if possible the instrument itself (for example, an mbira, an instrument from Zimbabwe). Ask students if they know what the instrument is. If they do not know immediately, what can they learn from looking at the picture? What part of the world is it likely to be from? How does it make a sound? What is the container it sits in made of, and what is its purpose? Through discussing the image they can learn a lot about the mystery instrument.

Trench warfare

Subject: History
Level: Key Stage 3

At the beginning or end of a lesson on trench warfare, write the following number on the board: 20 million. Challenge students to consider what it might represent, in relation to the topics they have been covering. The answer is that this is an estimate of the number of combined military and civilian deaths during World War 1.

Humanitarian law

Subject: Citizenship
Level: Key Stage 3 or 4

The British Red Cross give a very powerful example of a 'Guess the mystery object' activity. In the education section of their website (www.redcross.org.uk) you can find a picture of a small, green, plastic-looking object which you can show to your class. While looking like a toy, the object is a landmine, and is a good way to introduce a lesson on humanitarian law in Citizenship.

Sequence it

Give students a number of sentences which describe different stages in a process or sequence of events. Ask them to sequence the sentences into the correct order. When they have, ask them to explain why they chose the sequence they did.

This activity works well as revision of a historical chain of events, or steps in a process, which students have already studied.

Variations

- If the steps are clearly causal or must inevitably lead from one to another, then this activity can also be used for a sequence of events or a process which students have not yet studied. Rather than recalling the order, students figure out from the information in the sentences themselves the order in which they go, and uncover the details of the process or events described.

- As an additional activity, ask students to suggest a sentence or stage to go at the beginning or end of the existing sequence (i.e. to lengthen the sequence). This activity also works for a sequence of pictures (photos or drawings).

Examples

Gas exchange

Subject: Biology
Level: Key Stage 3

Biology students could sequence the following sentences to help them revise the process of gas exchange in the body:

a) Air moves down one of the two bronchi, into bronchioles and then into alveoli.
b) Air is exhaled, containing more carbon dioxide and less oxygen.
c) Movement of the ribs, rib muscles and diaphragm cause air to be inhaled through the mouth and nose.
d) Oxygen from the air dissolves in the moist lining and diffuses into the blood in small capillaries.
e) Air passes into the lungs through the trachea.

Answers: c, e, a, d, b.

Coasts

Subject: Geography
Level: Key Stage 3

Ask students studying coastlines to sequence the following five drawings. They illustrate the formation of arches, stacks and stumps. When they have worked out the correct answer, ask them to describe the features they can see in each of the drawings and what causes the changes in the coastline.

Sequence these pictures of cliff erosion:

Answer: 5, 3, 2, 4, 1.

Cloze this

A cloze activity is one where the student has to select words to complete a text in which blanks have been left.

Create a paragraph which sums up the learning from the lesson or the previous lesson. List the missing words (not in order) at the bottom of the handout or projection. Ask students to select the missing word for each blank space.

Variations

- To make this activity harder, list more words at the bottom than there are spaces in the text – some of the words are 'red herrings'. Alternatively, do not provide the missing words at all – students must decide on the most appropriate word without any prompt.

- Miss out whole phrases instead of individual words – so that students essentially have to finish the sentence rather than replace the missing word. In this case you may want to be more flexible on the answer, allowing for variations in the ways in which students phrase the end of the sentence.

Examples

Islam

Subject: Religious Education
Level: Key Stage 4

Below is a possible cloze activity on Islamic views on relationships. Students do not have a list of words to choose from, and so must think about what they have learned.

Islam has very strict views on love and sex.

Islam has very strict views on love and sex. These come from passages in the _____and _____ (sayings of the Prophet _____). Muslims see sexual intercourse as an act of _____ that fulfils human _____ and physical needs as well as creating children. Sexual intercourse is a gift from_____ and must only be between two people who are _____ .

Magnetic fields

Subject: Physics
Level: Key Stage 3

Project or write the following paragraph on the board at the end of a lesson on magnetic fields. Give students three minutes to decide which of the missing words (a–e) goes in which of the spaces (1–5).

Magnets create magnetic _____1_____ spaces around the magnet where magnetic materials are affected by forces. The magnetic field is strongest at the _____2_____of a magnet. These magnetic fields mean that _____3_____ poles attract, and _____4_____ poles _____5_____.

Missing words: a) like; b) fields; c) poles; d) unlike; d) repel.

What happens next?

Show students a sequence of events in pictures or words. Ask them to guess what will happen next and why. They will need to use their understanding of the process, and rules or patterns they have learned, to predict the next step.

Variations

- This activity also works for sequences of events that have already happened, but for which students do not yet know the next step in the historical chain of events. Ask students to use their knowledge of the context and individuals involved to guess what they think happened next.

- You could use this activity in conjunction with 'Sequence it' on page 90. Once students have sequenced a set of statements, ask them to predict what the next step or stage would be.

Examples

Experiments

Subject: Biology
Level: Key Stage 3

Prediction is often used in science experiments in the form of hypothesis writing. For example, students investigating the starch contents of food learn that iodine forms an intense blue-black coloured complex with starch. In the laboratory, students are often asked to test a number of foodstuffs for starch. Before adding a drop of iodine solution to each food sample (for example potato, apple, cheese) students can predict the colour that the iodine will turn, and explain why.

Elements of music

Subject: Music
Level: Key Stage 4

Play students a short piece of music on the keyboard or piano – either the first few bars of a sequence or a repeated ostinato. Ask for volunteers to sing you the next few notes: the sequence at a higher pitch, or the repeated notes of the ostinato, respectively. Ask students to name the device being used.

Cold War

Subject: History
Level: Key Stage 4

Show students studying the early years of the Cold War the summary table below, which shows American and Soviet actions. Can they see a pattern? What do they think might happen in the final box?

American response

1947: Announcement of Truman doctrine and Marshall plan.

1948: America and Britain announced that they wanted to create the new country of West Germany, and on 23 June they introduced a new currency.

1949: NATO formed.

Soviet response

1947: International conference organized to condemn Truman doctrine and Marshall plan. Communist workers told to strike to wreck Marshall plan.

1949: Comecon, a trading organization of communist countries, set up.

1948-9: The Berlin Blockade.

1949: The Formation of East Germany.

?

Odd word out

This activity is a quick starter or plenary that gets students thinking at the start of the lesson or brings together what they have been learning about at the end. Write or project four words on the board, all key words or words related to the topic. Three of the words should be related to each other in some way. The fourth should be the 'odd one out', not falling into the same category, though it can be related to one or more of the words in a different way.

Ask students to identify which word is the 'odd word out', either writing down their answer or putting up their hand. Which did they pick? Why?

Two or three 'odd word out' puzzles, one after the other, make a good length starter or plenary.

Variations

- Having shown students an example, ask them to try writing their own 'odd word out' puzzle. Ask for volunteers to read out or write their puzzle on the board for the rest of the class to figure out.

- This activity also works for sentences (spot the sentence that does not match) and pictures (odd photo out).

Examples

Glaciation

Subject: Geography
Level: Key Stage 4

Three 'odd word out' sets for a plenary towards the end of a unit on glaciation might be:

1. Corrie, Striation, Drumlin, U-shaped valley

2. Till, Esker, Drumlin, Outwash plain

3. V-shaped valley, Hanging valley, Arete, Pyramidal peak

Answers:

1. Drumlin – this is a feature created by glacial deposition, the others are features created by glacial erosion.

2. Till – this is the generic name for material deposited by a glacier, the other terms are for specific features of deposition.

3. V-shaped valley – this is a feature created by a river, the others are features created by a glacier.

Animal vocabulary

Subject: French
Level: Key Stage 3

These three 'odd word out' word sets could be used to revise animals names:

1. le cobaye, le chou, le chien, le lapin

2. le tigre, l'éléphant, le chat, la vache

3. le cheval, la souris, la vache, le cochon

Answers:

1. Le chou – this is a cabbage, all the others are animals.

2. Le chat – the only animal in this list commonly kept as a pet.

3. La souris – a tiny animal compared with the others in the list.

Writing styles

Subject: English language
Level: Key Stage 3

Challenge students studying writing styles to select the 'odd sentence out' from the following:

'Excuse me, please may I have my tea with two sugars.'
'If it wouldn't be too much trouble, I would also very much like a biscuit.'
'Lovely cuppa!'
'Yes, that would be sufficient milk, thank you.'

Ranking

Challenge students, in pairs, to rank a set of statements from most to least important. This activity is similar to the 'Sequence it' activity on page 90. However, the big difference is that, instead of putting statements into a sequence according to stages of a process or chain of events, students put the statements in order according to which they think are most important or significant.

This activity explores students' opinions, and there is generally not a right or wrong answer. Instead it encourages students to weigh up different causal factors, needs or opinions. As a result, the debrief is as important as the activity itself. Ask students which statement they ranked first. Which did they rank last? Why did they choose this statement? What do other groups think about this choice? Did anyone put a different statement first? Why?

Variations

- This activity can be carried out by listing all the statements on the board or on a handout, and asking students to write the 'ranking' next to each sentence. So they would write '1' next to the item they think is most important, '2' next to the second most important, and so on.

- Create a pack of cards for each pair, with a statement printed on each card. Ask students to rearrange these cards into a vertical line, putting the most important at the top and the least important at the bottom. This approach allows students to physically move the statements, and experiment with different ranking.

- A diamond nine ranking gives students some flexibility in their ranking. They must choose a sentence to rank first and last. However, by arranging their cards in a diamond shape, the second row down contains two cards of equal importance, the third three, and the fourth two again. If more than nine cards are involved, ask students to leave out entirely the least important card(s).

Examples

Human rights

Subject: Citizenship
Level: Key Stage 3

Ask students to rank their human rights in a diamond nine ranking. Which right do they think it is most important to protect? Which rights are less essential? You can see a possible ranking in the diagram opposite (note that the students who created this ranking had already chosen to leave out some rights so that they had nine remaining). There is obviously no right answer to this, and the aim is to get students thinking (and arguing) about why each right is important, and understanding the interdependence of their rights.

This activity is adapted from an activity in K. Brown and S. Fairbrass (2009), *The Citizenship Teacher's Handbook*, London: Continuum.

How would you rank your rights?

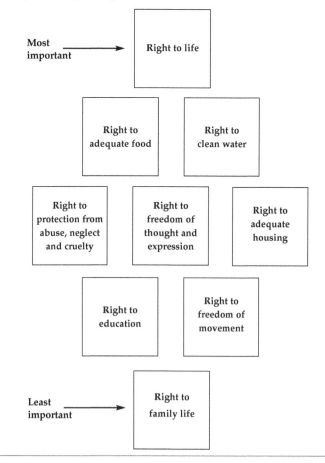

The Treaty of Versailles

Subject: History
Level: Key Stage 4

Create packs of the nine cards below for each pair or group of students. Write the following statement onto the board: 'It was difficult for Clemenceau, Lloyd George and Wilson to reach their aims in the peace talks'. Which of their cards do they think best explains why this was the case? Which is least significant/relevant? Can they rank the cards in a diamond nine according to their order of importance? If they can think of another reason, they should add it on a spare card, and can use it to replace one of the existing nine.

British and French public opinion was strongly anti-German.

Wilson decided to compromise because he believed he could use the League of Nations to fix any problems with the treaty afterwards.

Their different political viewpoints (self-determination v. imperialism) made it difficult for them all to be happy.

They could not always agree, for example, on the level of reparations.

Clemenceau, 'the Tiger', argued fiercely.

Their different experiences of the war made it impossible for them all to be happy.

Wilson and Lloyd George sided at times against Clemenceau, but with different motives (LG because he wanted to stop France being too powerful, W because he had strong ideals).

Lloyd George recommended moderation to both the other leaders.

Wilson was too idealistic — he didn't understand the difficulties of self-determination in Europe.

Spot the difference

Project two photographs or pictures onto the board or distribute copies to students. Can they spot the difference or differences between the two images? How would they describe these differences?

In most cases, the more important question comes next: How can you explain these differences? What has changed between the two images to bring about the change? How do these differences relate to what students learned about last lesson?

Variations

- This activity also works well using two graphs that describe different situations.

- For a simple version, present two images, but with only one difference. For example, the apparatus for an experiment in Biology, but with one piece of equipment missing or wrongly assembled.

- For a more nuanced version, ask students to identify similarities between two images as well as differences, for example between two paintings of the same landscape by different artists. This becomes a more complex compare and contrast activity.

Examples

Population

Subject: Geography
Level: Key Stage 4

Give Geography students learning to analyse population pyramids the two pyramids on the next page.

What differences can students spot between the two pyramids? Ask students to describe the differences in structure, and what this tells them about the population. For example, pyramid A has a much narrower base, indicating a lower birth rate. Pyramid A is narrower in the older age groups, indicating a lower life expectancy. Pyramid B has, overall, longer bars, indicating a larger population.

Tell students that these pyramids are in fact two possible pyramids for the same country, constructed from two population projections. What factor might bring about the lower birth rate, lower life expectancy, and smaller overall population shown in Pyrmaid A? They may guess war, famine and disease – the answer is AIDS.

Spot the differences between the population pyramids:

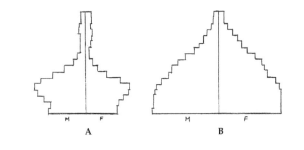

A   B

Glaciaton

Subject: Geography
Level: Key Stage 3

Show students two photos or drawings of a valley. One should be of a V-shaped river valley (A), the other of a U-shaped glacial valley (B). Can students spot the differences between the two images? They might point out that the interlocking spurs in valley A have become truncated in B. Tributary streams to the main river in A have been stranded in hanging valleys, creating waterfalls, in valley B. The V-shape of the valley in A has become U-shaped in B.

Subject: Biology
Level: Key Stage 3

Show students the following table of components in two samples of air:

Gas	Sample 1	Sample 2
Oxygen	21 per cent	17 per cent
Carbon dioxide	0.04 per cent	4 per cent

What are the differences between the two samples? Encourage them to use the data to illustrate their answers e.g. there is a hundred times more carbon dioxide in Sample 2 compared to Sample 1. What could explain the differences between the two samples? Where/when might they have been taken?

Answer: Sample 1 is air as it is inhaled by a person, and Sample 2 as it is exhaled.

Sort these

Give each pair or group of students a set of cards. On each card is a key word, a term, a phrase or a viewpoint. Explain to students that these cards fall into different categories. Explain what these categories are. They might specifically relate to the topic like those below:

- Less Economically Developed Country

- More Economically Developed Country

- Passé

- Composé

- Imparfait

- Christianity

- Islam

- Both religions

Alternatively, categories might be more generic, such as:

- True

- Generally true

- False

- In favour

- Against

Give students a limited amount of time to read and sort the cards into piles for each category.

Variations

- Use images instead of words on the cards.

- Distribute a couple of blank cards in each pack, and challenge students who finish sorting quickly to think of their own words or terms to add to one or more of the categories.

- This activity could be carried out as a whole class activity using an interactive whiteboard. Divide part of the board into areas to represent the categories, and distribute the words or phrases across the rest of the board. Ask a student to come to the front and drag one of the listed words or phrases into the category he or she thinks it belongs in. Do other students agree with this categorization? Repeat.

- Challenge students to create their own categories. Distribute the words, terms or phrases as above, and tell students that they fall into a number of different categories. Their job is to suggest what the categories might be, and then to sort the cards according to their suggestion. How well does their categorization work? Now that they have sorted all the cards, are there any that do not fit their suggested categories? Can they now think of a better way to group the cards?

Examples

Places

Subject: French
Level: Key Stage 3

Distribute cards, like those below, to each pair or group of students. 'Quels pays connaissez-vous?'. Ask students to sort the cards into the countries they have, between them, visited, and those they have not. Give them the following prompts for discussing with their partner, and for feedback to class:

Je connais le/la/les ...
Je suis allé(e) à/au/en/aux ...

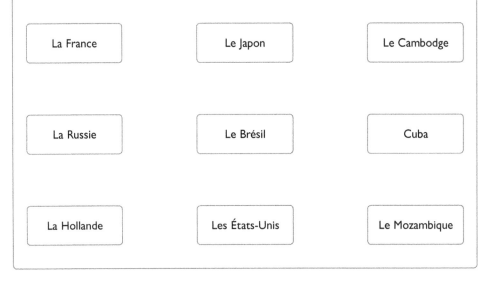

La France	Le Japon	Le Cambodge
La Russie	Le Brésil	Cuba
La Hollande	Les États-Unis	Le Mozambique

Should Britain adopt the Euro?

Subject: Citizenship
Level: Key Stage 4

Create a set of cards, like those below, for each group. Ask students to sort the cards into two categories:

- Arguments for Britain adopting the Euro.

- Arguments against Britain adopting the Euro.

If we have the Euro, then it means that Britain will not be able to set its own interest rates. Britain might need low interest rates at a time when the rest of Europe needs higher ones. This might create problems for our economy.

Having the same currency makes it easier for countries to trade with each other. If Britain does not adopt the Euro, then we will find it harder to trade with those countries that do.

Although we have not joined the Euro, our economy has grown well.

The Euro makes it a lot easier to compare prices. You can work out if something would cost you less in another country, so it is easier to get bargains.

The Euro would make things easier for Britons going to Europe. They would not have to change their money from pounds into Euros. Each time you change your money you have to pay a commission, so it would save them money.

If we join the Euro then we will be less independent. We might have our rates of tax set by the EU.

Since the Euro has been introduced, the economies of European countries have not grown quickly.

Lots of foreign companies invest in Britain. For example, they build factories here, which creates jobs and prosperity. If we do not adopt the Euro, then these companies might invest in EU countries that do have the Euro. Britain would lose out.

If we do not join the Euro then we will not be as heavily involved in the EU as we could be. This might mean that we lose influence: we might have no say in important decisions that affect us.

Finish this sentence

Students must match the first and second halves of a number of sentences.

Prepare by writing some sentences relating to the topic of the lesson. Then chop these sentences in half, mixing up the order of the second halves so that they are not in the same order as the first halves.

Give students a list of the 'first halves' and 'second halves' and ask them to complete the sentences. They can either draw a line between matching 'halves' or list the number/letters of the two halves of each pair (e.g. 1d, 2a etc.).

Variations

- Rather than distributing the sentences on a worksheet, project the two lists of sentence 'halves' and pick a student from the class to come up to the board and draw a line between the two halves of a matching pair. Repeat, asking a different student to complete each sentence.

- To make this activity easier, divide the sentences in such a way that it is possible to select the second half based on the grammar of the sentence alone: all but the correct match is nonsensical as well as factually incorrect. To make it harder, ensure that, in terms of the grammar of the sentences, each 'first half' could match with more than one 'second half'. Students have to understand the material to finish the sentence rather than relying on the sentence making sense grammatically.

- This activity can work as a card sort for students to solve in pairs. For this version, you will need to create a pack of cards for each pair, with half a sentence typed on each card. Students physically match the two ends of each sentence.

- Instead of two halves of a sentence, students could match a number with its corresponding description, or a picture with its corresponding caption.

- If the sentences form some kind of sequence or describe a process, you could ask students to order the sentences once they have been matched (see 'Sequence it', on page 90).

Examples

The Corn Laws

Subject: History
Level: Key Stage 4

Ask students to match the two halves of the following sentences, and then put the full sentences in order to form a paragraph explaining the introduction of the Corn Laws:

1. British farmers made a lot of money during

2. The Corn Laws stopped wheat from abroad being sold in Britain

3. Farmers feared that when the war ended cheap wheat from

4. Since lots of rich landowning farmers were also MPs

   a) if the price of wheat fell below 80 shillings a quarter.

   b) the French wars when Napoleon stopped wheat from entering Britain.

   c) they forced Parliament to pass new Corn Laws.

   d) Europe would force down the high prices they were charging.

Questionnaire design

Subject: Maths
Level: Key Stage 4

Ask students to match the following sentence 'halves' to revise their learning on questionnaire design:

1. Questionnaires are one way of collecting data

2. Questionnaires can be carried out in a number of ways including

3. Questionnaire questions should be

   a) by phone, post, via the internet or in person.

   c) clear and unbiased.

   b) from a large number of people.

Treaty of Versailles

Subject: History
Level: Key Stage 4

Challenge students to match the following numbers with what they represent. All numbers relate to the terms of the Versailles treaty.

1. 100,000

2. 15

3. 132

4. 440

    a) The number of years the Saar region was given to the French.

    b) The number of articles in the Versailles treaty.

    c) The maximum number of soldiers the German army could have.

    d) The number of billion gold marks reparations were later set at.

Analogies

The term 'analogy' has different meanings in different fields of study. In Biology two anatomical structures are said to be *analogous* when they serve similar functions but are not evolutionarily related, and in Maths some types of analogy have a precise mathematical formulation. Broader comparisons are also sometimes referred to as analogies: 'God is like the sun'; 'The heart is like a pump'. The idea of analogies like these is to draw out similarities to explain something unknown through something known. They are often used in teaching to provide students with insight.

Another form of analogy, that you and your students may not have come across but which can also be useful in the classroom, formally compares two pairs which have the same relationship. A classic example of this type of analogy is as follows: Hand is to palm as foot is to sole. This is sometimes written Hand : Palm :: Foot : Sole. Other simple analogies include:

Day : sun :: night : moon.
Puppy : dog :: kitten : cat.

Create an analogy specific to the topic that students are learning about. It often works well if one of the pairs is formed of people, events, processes or objects from the lesson, and the other pair describes a more familiar relationship from everyday life. Remove one of the four words and then write up the incomplete analogy on the board. Give students a time limit in which to suggest, individually or in pairs, a word or term to complete the incomplete pair. Remind them that the key to solving the analogy is to work out the relationship between the complete pair of words. Then they need to think of a word that completes a similar relationship in the other pair. Students may not finish the analogy in the way you had in mind, instead drawing out another element of the relationship described. The important thing is that they can explain why they chose the word they did. What are the similarities in the relationships within the first and second pairs?

Variations

- A good way to introduce analogies to students, and a good starter or plenary in its own right, is to display a complete formal analogy. Explain the format to students (perhaps using one of the simple analogies above). Next, ask students to use their understanding of the topic to explain the subject-specific analogy you have created. What is the relationship within each of the two pairs?

- Students who quickly complete the analogy could try to create their own, either starting from a single pair you provide, or choosing their own pair from within a topic and thinking of similar relationships outside the subject.

- When students have got the hang of explaining analogies and writing their own, ask them to consider the limitations of analogies. In what ways do the relationships within the two pairs differ from each other? What would lead the analogy to break down?

Examples

My family

Subject: French
Level: Key Stage 3

Challenge students to complete these three analogies in three minutes.

La tante: l'oncle :: la mère : ?

La soeur : le frère :: la nièce : ?

Le grand-père : le petit-fils :: le grand-oncle : ?

Photosynthesis

Subject : Biology
Level : Key Stage 3

Write this analogy on the board for students to read as they come into class. Open the lesson by asking if anyone can suggest a missing word.

Chocolate: you :: ? : a green plant.

Take a few answers and discuss which one works the best. What provides green plants energy in the way in which a chocolate bar provides energy for you? Where does the analogy break down – what is the difference between how we get our energy and how plants get theirs?

Section 6
Physical

Stand on the line

This is a great activity for any topic which involves students' opinions. It gets them out of their seats and physically indicating their opinion. This means that every student has to think about his or her own view, even those who are reticent to express it orally.

Move desks so there is enough space for students to stand along one side of the classroom. Read or project a statement such as: 'Young people who commit crimes should be harshly punished'; 'Darcy is the character who demonstrates the most prejudice'; 'It is possible to have a Just War'.

Invite a few students, or all the class, to stand along an imaginary line (a 'values continuum line') running from 'Strongly agree' at one side of the room to 'Strongly disagree' at the other, with 'Neither agree nor disagree' right in the middle. If you have time beforehand, you can prepare signs to indicate the ends of the continuum.

Ask some students why they are standing where they are. 'Because Dan did', or 'I don't know' are not acceptable answers. Emphasize that as they hear their peers' opinions, they are free to change theirs and move along the line, but when they move they may have to explain why; whose arguments have convinced them?

'Stand on the line' can work well as a starter to move into a discussion, or as a stimulus for a piece of written work in which students justify their position on the continuum.

Variations

- If it is logistically difficult to get students moving around, they can mark their opinions on a worksheet version of the values continuum. The down side of this is that a mark in pen is more difficult to change than a physical position in the classroom – it is more difficult for students to respond flexibly as they hear the opinions of others.

- You can create a semi-permanent values continuum if you want to refer back to it. Ask students to write their opinions on paper, provide them with clothes pegs and then invite them to hang their opinions on a 'values washing-line', a string running across the classroom. The washing-line can then remain in place for the next few lessons, and provide the focus for subsequent starters and plenaries when you could give students the opportunity to edit and/or move their opinion along the line. (This is adapted from an idea by Brian Jacobs, a Citizenship teacher at Cedar Mount High School in Manchester, described in K. Brown and S. Fairbrass (2009), *The Citizenship Teacher's Handbook*, London: Continuum.)

Examples

Introduction to Citizenship

Subject: Citizenship
Level: Key Stage 3

The worksheet below is a values continuum worksheet introducing students to the topics they will cover in Citizenship lessons.

How much do you agree or disagree? Read through the statements and mark your view on the scale.

Strongly agree Not sure Strongly disagree

Newspapers should not publish stories about Britney's personal life

A child who kills someone should be treated the same as an adult should

All children must attend school even if it conflicts with their parents' beliefs

The BBC news always tells the truth

I have a responsibility to help people in less developed countries

The UK should swap the Pound for the Euro

I can say what I want about anything

When I reach 18 I will make sure I vote at elections

Violence never helps in finding solutions to problems

I know my rights if I buy something that is faulty

How British you are can be judged by your colour and religion

I would boycott a company because of the way it treats the people it employs

I am not swayed by advertising

This country should allow more asylum seekers to live here

Children younger than 13 should be allowed to work

There should be a fine if you do not recycle your drinks can

I could make a difference in my community: what I think matters

I am good at working with others and listening to their views

Act this out

A quick and fun starter or plenary in which one student acts out a word, process, or action for the rest of the class to guess. Although it can seem fairly frivolous, this activity sticks in students' minds, and as a result so does the information conveyed.

Beforehand, you will need to prepare by thinking of actions, names, titles or other terms relevant to the lesson and suitable for acting out. Ask for a volunteer and hand them one of the folded pieces of paper or cards on which you have written a word or term. Give them a few moments to think, and then ask them to act out what is written on the card.

Students who think they know the answer should put their hand up, and wait for you to pick them. Meanwhile the student 'acting' should carry on until the class guess the correct answer – the student may have to repeat his or her actions, or think of another way to act out the word. They must not speak or gesticulate when they hear nearly the right answer!

When someone has guessed the correct answer, draw out their thinking. What elements of the dramatic performance led the student to guess correctly? Why? How does the term link to the topic? What is the definition of the word?

Variations

- Like other starters and plenaries that involve guessing a word (such as Pictionary™, page 72, and Taboo™, page 78) this activity can be played as a team game. You will need to prepare several cards with key terms written on them, and divide students into two teams. Pick a student from each team to act. One student goes first, and only their team can guess the term. Pick a student from the opposite team to time one or two minutes, and challenge the first team to guess the term from their team members' acting in that time. If they do, they get a point. Repeat the process for the other team, and as many times as you have prepared cards.

- This activity only works for fairly simple actions or terms. However, if you want to extend it to more compound terms, book titles or more complex process names, you can use the well-known acting game 'Charades'. Students use gestures to indicate information about the phrase, and act out elements of it. There are many variations in the gestures used; you might want to follow your own or use the ones in the table below.

Meaning	Gesture
Number of words	Hold the corresponding number of fingers up
The word you are working on	Hold the corresponding fingers up
Number of syllables in the word	Lay the corresponding number of fingers on your arm
The syllable you are working on	Lay the corresponding fingers on your arm
'Sounds like'	Cup your hand below your ear
'The'	Form your hands into a capital T shape
'A'	Place your fingertips together to form a tent shape

Examples

Coasts

Subject: Geography
Level: Key Stage 3

Geography students learn about the power of waves to shape the coast. There are two main categories of waves, with different features: constructive and destructive.

Pick a volunteer, and give them a piece of folded paper with either the word 'constructive' or 'destructive' written on it. Ask them to convey their wave type, using the medium of mime. Constructive waves are long and low, and have a strong swash going up the beach and a weak backwash coming back down. Destructive waves are shorter and higher, and have a weaker swash relative to their strong backwash.

Indicate an area of the classroom floor which represents the beach, and challenge the student to 'be' a constructive or destructive wave. Encourage the rest of the class to guess, and then explain their answer with reference to the features of the wave.

The Tempest

Subject: English Literature
Level: Key Stage 3

Students studying *The Tempest* need to be able to identify the main characters in the text. Having spent time studying their key extracts and the characters, 'Act this out' can work well as a fun starter or plenary.

Pick a student and give them a name of a character in the play. Ask the student to spend 30 seconds or a minute in the character of that person, giving as much information as they can about the character through what they do and how they move, but without speaking. Challenge the rest of the class to guess which character they are, and then to explain their answer, with reference to what they know about the role, status, disposition and habits of the character.

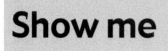

Show me

This is a more active version of 'True or false?' (page 26), or 'Sort these' (page 104). The idea is that you read out a figure, fact, or statement, or show a picture to students and they 'show' you which category they think it falls into, whether that is 'true' or 'false', 'Christianity' or 'Islam'.

To show you, each student will need a card for each category. Laminated and/or coloured cards are clear and last well. When they have heard the phrase or seen the picture, they hold up the card that they think best corresponds.

This activity is great for kinaesthetic learners and to wake up sleepy classes. Every student has to have a go at answering the question, and with everyone answering they can immediately be corrected without being singled out. You can get a sense of how well the class as a whole, and individual students, have understood the topic.

Variations

- Mini-whiteboards work well for this activity. Ask students to write the titles of the two categories you have selected in large letters on each side of the whiteboard. When you have read out a phrase, they have to hold up the whiteboard with the correct category facing you.

- If you have neither mini-whiteboards nor laminated cards, you could simply allocate a hand to each of the categories. For example: 'Hold up your right hand if you think the statement is false: hold up your left hand if you think the statement is true'.

- If you are concerned that students are simply looking at the answers of others before having a go at answering themselves, you can ask them to raise their cards or hands together at the end of a time limit.

Examples

Textiles

Subject: Design and Technology
Level: Key Stage 4

Ask students to write 'Synthetic' on one side of their mini-whiteboard, and 'Natural' on the other. Name a textile, and ask students to hold up their board to indicate if it is natural or synthetic. The list might include: cotton; viscose; linen; silk; acrylic; polyester; wool; nylon. To make the activity a step harder, show students a picture of a material and ask them to identify from the picture whether it is natural or synthetic. Ask a student who gets the answer right to identify the specific textile.

Take the activity a step further, and ask students to change the categories on their whiteboard. Choose categories depending on the aspect you want students to revise, for example 'Warm' and 'Cool', or 'Durable' and 'Not durable'. Repeat the list of textiles, and ask students to show you which category they think the textile falls into.

Development

Subject: Geography
Level: Key Stage 3

Give students a laminated A4 card each, with 'UK' written on one side, and 'Senegal' on the other. Read out the following facts, and ask students to show you whether they think the statement is about the UK or Senegal.

1. The life expectancy is 79 years *(UK)*.

2. 1.4 per cent of the population is involved in farming for their work *(UK)*.

3. 40 per cent of those over 15 can read and write *(Senegal)*.

4. 99 per cent of those over 15 can read and write *(UK)*.

5. On average, each woman has 4.86 children *(Senegal)*.

6. The life expectancy is 57 years *(Senegal)*.

7. The birth rate is 37 births per 1,000 members of the population per year (a high birth rate) *(Senegal)*.

8. 4 per cent of the population live below the poverty line *(UK)*.

9. On average, each woman has 1.66 children *(UK)*.

10. 77.5 per cent of people are involved in farming for their work *(Senegal)*.

Section 7

Reflect on your learning

Traffic lights

How well have your students understood the lesson, concept, topic or process? Display a picture or photograph of a set of traffic lights: red, amber and green. A green light represents a solid and comfortable understanding of the topic: a student choosing a green light feels that he or she has 'got it'. A student who chooses amber has understood some or most of the material, but is not totally confident in using his or her understanding to answer questions or in applying a new skill. A red light indicates that a student does not feel that he or she has got to grips with the topic at all. It may help to write a word or two next to each of the three coloured lights to remind students what they represent.

Ask students to decide which light they think best represents their understanding of the lesson or topic. Explain that this is not a test, and that you are not going to be recording what students say, so they should be honest about their understanding. Then go through the lights: red, amber and green, and ask students to raise their hands to indicate the colour they have chosen for themselves.

This activity is a form of assessment for learning. Encouraging students to reflect on what they have understood can enable them to take more ownership of their learning and identify the areas that they need to work more on. It can also help you to assess how well you have taught a topic. You can quickly see which students need more support, including students who otherwise might keep their head down in class and remain unidentified for much longer.

You can use the results of the 'Traffic lights' activity to plan and differentiate subsequent activities: ask students to collect worksheets corresponding to the colour they selected (the green worksheet extending students with a good understanding, the red worksheet reinforcing key points or skills). Alternatively, ask students to pair or team up, each 'red' student pairing with a 'green'. For a short activity, give the student with a good understanding five minutes to explain the topic, in their own words, to the student who is unclear on this material. Or keep students in these 'mixed traffic light' teams for the next activity or lesson. Incorporating an element of 'peer teaching' in this way often means that you can get the whole class to green much more quickly than if you worked individually with each 'red light' student. Students may also explain the material in a way their peers find more accessible, and feel positive about their role as 'teacher'.

Variations

- Teachers who use this approach regularly could choose to give students pieces of laminated card in red, orange and green which they can hold up to indicate their understanding.

- If you have mini-whiteboards, ask each student to draw the appropriate coloured circle onto their whiteboard (if they have coloured whiteboard pens), or to write the word red, amber or green onto their board before holding it up.

- Carry out the traffic light activity at the beginning and end of a topic. At the beginning, it will give you a sense of students' existing understanding. Ask them to record in the margin or the back of their books the colour they chose. Repeat the activity at the end of the topic. Then ask who has changed colour. Who has moved towards a green? Has anyone moved in the other direction?

- An alternative scale to 'red, amber and green' is '0–5'. Five fingers held up indicate that a student is very confident about their understanding of a topic; no fingers means they have not understood at all. Ask the class to raise a hand, holding up the number of fingers between zero and five which they feel best reflects their understanding.

Example

Map skills

Subject: Geography
Level: Key Stage 3

Some Year 7 Geography students have used six-figure grid references before; others have not. This can give a lot of variation in class between those who can give and read references easily, and those who are confused, particularly about the third and sixth digits. Having introduced this skill and given students some opportunity to practice, ask them to identify themselves as a red, amber or green light. Pair or team those who are struggling with six-figure grid references with those who are confident.

Ask each pair to create five or ten clues for a grid reference test. Some questions should ask for the symbol or feature found at a given grid reference, and some questions should ask for the grid reference of an easily identifiable feature. They must work out the answers, but write them on a separate piece of paper. Each pair can then swap tests with another pair, and answer the questions, before swapping their answers back to be marked by the group that set them. The question setting and question answering provides two opportunities for the 'green light' student to work through the answers with the 'red light' student. At the end, ask who feels as though they have moved further towards green.

Set a target

'How can I improve my work?' This activity encourages students to think about and provide answers to this question, identifying a specific and achievable target for improvement. Without activities like this, which help students identify good practice, many students may not be aware of what they could, or should, be doing to improve their work.

Having marked and handed back a piece of homework, group project work, test or results of an oral presentation, give students time to read through your comments. Ask them to identify what they could have done better, and to write a target for their next piece of work.

Variations

- Your class may find it easier to choose a target from a list rather than write their own. After marking a test, project or homework, make a note of comments you find yourself writing regularly on students' work: 'Look at the number of marks available and try and make the corresponding number of points'; 'Reference all secondary material you include'; 'Read the question!' These will obviously vary, depending on the kind of work. Compile a list of these reoccurring comments, and display or distribute them to students. Explain what you mean by each of the comments, and then ask students to identify which they think applies to them. Ask them to select the target they think is most appropriate and achievable for them.

- If you use this activity regularly, you could provide students with a 'target form', perhaps glued into the inside cover of their exercise book or folder. Allow columns for the date, the target and a 'follow up' column. Ask students to record their target and the date they set it. When they have completed or had their next piece of work marked, ask them to reflect on whether they achieved their target. They could write a comment in the 'follow up' column, or give themselves a score out of five (0 = made no progress towards target; 5 = fully achieved target). They can then set themselves a target for the next piece of work – either repeating the same target, or selecting a new one.

- Vary the kind of target students set: ask them to focus on presentation one week ('I will draw graphs in pencil'); content the next ('I will include examples in my answers'). Alternatively, rather than focusing on a specific piece of written work, ask students to reflect on their approach to class. Display a list of targets for positive learning: this might include, 'I will bring the books I need to each lesson'; 'I will put my hand up and ask if I don't understand'; 'I will put my hand up if I want to make a point'. Ask students to select a target for the lesson, or the week. At the end of the lesson, ask students to consider the extent to which they achieved their target.

- Rather than setting a target for themselves, put students in pairs, and ask them to select a target for their peer. This could be in any of the formats mentioned above.

Examples

Exam practice

Subject: History
Level: Key Stage 4

Below are comments written on Year 11 History practice exam questions. Each comment has been translated into a suggested target for the mock exam. Students can choose from these, or write one of their own.

Comment	Possible target
The question says 'up to 1932' – this is correct information but much later chronologically, so you do not get any marks	I will read the question carefully
Spell out what you mean here, even if it seems obvious	I will explain fully each point that I make
There are six marks available for this question, but you have only made two points	I will look at the marks available for each question and adapt the length and depth of my answer
I can't read your writing here!	I will take time to write clearly and legibly
This is true, but what happened that shows this?	I will back up each point I make with evidence

Various

Subject: Citizenship
Level: Key Stage 3

Below is the 'target form' of a Year 9 Citizenship student, complete with their first few targets from the year.

Date	Target	Did I achieve my target (5= completely; 0= not at all)
15.09.09	I will put forward my opinion more in class discussion	4
29.09.09	I will give a piece of information or evidence to back up my opinion when I give it	3
13.10.09	Before I write a bit of extended writing, I will draw a short plan of the points I will include	5

Self- or peer mark

Self- or peer assessment – marking your own or another student's work – is common practice for getting students evaluating their own progress and actively involved in the learning process. Self- or peer assessment can mean much more than just a few minutes at the start or end of a lesson: making sure students understand the mark scheme before they complete the work, giving students time to really evaluate larger pieces of work, and training students to provide constructive feedback all take time. However, once students are familiar with the process, and perhaps in addition to opportunities for more in-depth marking, peer or self-assessment work well as a starter or plenary.

A common approach to peer marking is to set a quick test at the start of a lesson ('Write the definitions for these key terms', 'Spell the following words correctly', etc.). When they are finished, instruct students to swap books and then mark their partners' work as you read out the answers. While students may benefit from going through the answers, peer or self-marking really comes into its own when students have to consider how good an answer is (rather than simply whether it is right or wrong). So, use this activity for marking questions that can elicit a range of different correct responses, with the focus on the quality of the explanation rather than the answer itself.

Successful peer or self-marking requires two things. First, a mark scheme. It is your role as teacher to make sure that students are clear on the criteria they are marking to. Are they focusing on content? Or should they take presentation into account? What should they look for in a good answer? Are there marks available for examples, for details, for naming individuals, places or events? You could use generic criteria that you use for all homework, criteria you have created specifically for this work; or if the question comes from an examination you can adapt the relevant mark scheme.

Second, students need to know how they should provide their feedback. Should they provide a grade (relating to mark bands you have given them), or comments, or both? Talk to students about what they think makes a helpful comment. You could introduce the idea of a feedback sandwich: two comments about positive aspects of the work sandwiching a point about something which could be improved.

Becoming familiar with mark schemes, identifying what gets marks and what does not and seeing some really good, as well as some less good, pieces of work, all help students become more aware of exactly how they can improve their own work.

Variations

- Other work which could be productively peer or self-assessed includes:

  - Essays or pieces of extended writing.

  - Diagrams or illustrations.

  - Creative writing.

  - Mnemonics, anagrams, acronyms and many of the other creative starter or plenary activities described in this book.

- Students could mark work completed during the lesson as a plenary, or at the start of the following lesson. Alternatively, they could mark work that has been completed for homework.

- For students new to the process, mark the same piece of work together. Distribute copies of a mock essay or an anonymized essay from a previous year group, and the corresponding mark scheme. Set each pair a different section to mark, or work through the different criteria together.

- Having set a piece of homework, a helpful plenary activity can be to show students the marking criteria and talk them through it. Give students the opportunity to ask any questions they have on how to achieve well.

- Better still, get students to write their own marking criteria. A really productive plenary when setting a piece of homework can be to ask students what they think this work should be marked on. Having explained the piece of work, compile students' ideas on what they need to do to get the marks available. This really encourages students to think about how to achieve well when they come to complete the work.

- Pick a student or ask for a volunteer for the 'hot seat'. Address five questions to this student, which they must try to answer. All other students in the class must write down (in the back of their book, or on mini-whiteboards), whether they think the answer given is right or wrong – they are effectively marking as they go along. If they think the answer is wrong, what would they have said instead? What would they have added for a better answer? Ask individual students for the mark they gave out of five. Or ask for feedback on what was answered well, and what could have been answered better.

Examples

Persuasive writing

Subject: English Language
Level: Key Stage 3

Students learning how to write persuasively were asked to write a letter for homework, persuading a friend to their point of view. At the lesson plenary, students were asked to suggest the marking criteria, based on what they had learned in the lesson on persuasive writing, and any other criteria they thought might be important for the homework. They came up with the following list, which they all wrote into their homework diaries:

To persuade the reader the letter must:

• Include repetition.

• Be personalized – what might persuade the particular individual?

• Use questions.

• Be emotional.

The letter should also be:

• About one side of A4.

• Typed up.

• Set out in an informal letter style.

At the start of the next lesson, students marked their partner's work, using the grid on the next page. They did not provide an overall mark, but did give a summary comment which followed the feedback sandwich format: something good about the work, something that could be improved, something else good about the work.

Criteria

Put a cross at the place on the scale that
best shows how each criterion was met.

Not at all ⟵——————⟶ A lot/completely

Includes repetition

Is personal
to the reader

Uses questions

Is emotional

Is about one
side of A4

Is typed

Is set out in an
informal letter style

Legal ages

Subject: Citizenship
Level: Key Stage 3

One student from a Year 8 class was picked to take the 'hot seat' and answer five questions. These questions and the student's answers are shown in the table below. The rest of the class were asked to mark the answers from the 'hot seat' in the back of their book – a tick if they thought the answer given was correct, across if not. If they thought the answer was wrong, they should also give the correct answer. The last column of the table shows one student's peer assessment of the answers. Her marking is right, except for the age at which you can buy fireworks, which is 18.

How old do you have to be to ...	Answer by student in 'hot seat'	One student marks the answers from the 'hot seat'
Go to the pub (but not drink alcohol)	14	√
Work full time	16	√
Buy fireworks	16	√
Be employed for a few hours each week	14	× 13
Own a house	21	× 18

Top tips

This activity helps your students think about what worked for them in getting to grips with a new skill. That might be calculating volume, measuring wind speed, using the passé composé or keeping safe in a laboratory. What advice would they give to someone about to start learning? Ask students, individually or in pairs, to put together their list of top tips. In deciding on what should go in their tips, students reflect on their new skill and what they think is particularly important, tricky or relevant.

Variations

• If the skill is one that students will use all year, such as how to measure distance on a map, or how to use a Bunsen burner safely, you could display the 'Top tips' around the classroom. Ask students to contribute their advice, and compile a single list on the board, adapting and adding points in response to students' ideas. Type or write these up for display. Alternatively, ask all students to present their tips for display in an eye-catching and clear format, and create a wall display.

• As well as giving advice on specific skills, you can use this activity to encourage students to consider what makes a good learner more generally. What tips would students give to, say, new Year 7 or Year 10 students on how to do well in Spanish, or Maths, or RE? What would they do differently if they started the year again? You might provide some examples to get students thinking, such as: 'Keep notes in order for when you come to revise'; 'Do your homework as soon as possible after the lesson so you remember what you have to do'; 'Put your opinion forward in class so that you can adapt it in response to feedback from your friends and the teacher'. While notionally these tips are being prepared for another class, they allow students in your class to think about themselves as learners.

Example

Annotation

Subject: Geography
Level: Key Stage 3

On the next page are some 'Top tips on annotating', written by a Year 9 Geography student at the end of a lesson on annotating photographs.

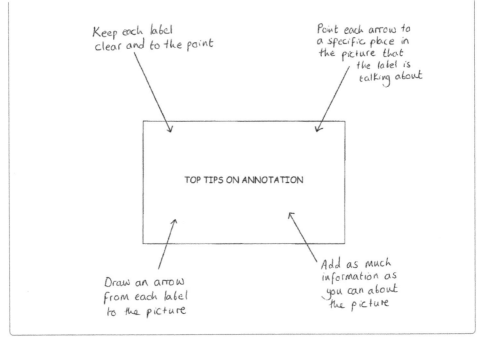

Keep each label clear and to the point

Point each arrow to a specific place in the picture that the label is talking about

TOP TIPS ON ANNOTATION

Draw an arrow from each label to the picture

Add as much information as you can about the picture

Various

Subject: German
Level: Key Stage 3

Some tips on how to do well in German, compiled by Year 8 German students:

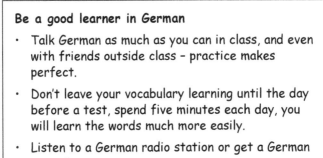

Be a good learner in German

- Talk German as much as you can in class, and even with friends outside class – practice makes perfect.
- Don't leave your vocabulary learning until the day before a test, spend five minutes each day, you will learn the words much more easily.
- Listen to a German radio station or get a German magazine.
- Don't worry about making mistakes, just have a go!

Link the learning

With learning in secondary school so clearly demarcated into subject areas and each subject area under pressure to 'get through' their curriculum and meet internal targets, it can be easy for teachers and students alike to forget the links between subjects. Not only that, but students may not be given the opportunity to make the connections between what they learn at school and the outside world.

A different and thought-provoking way to start a lesson, or productively use a few minutes at the end of a lesson, is to encourage students to 'link the learning'. Have they touched on this topic in any other subjects? What did they learn? Could they apply the material in this lesson to any other subject? What specific 'angle' does Geography, Citizenship or English provide on this topic? When might they actually use this skill outside of school? Decide which questions you want to focus on, and then write them on the board. Ask students to discuss their ideas in pairs, write down their ideas on mini-whiteboards or feed them back to the whole class.

Variations

- As homework, and to start the following lesson, ask students to keep their eyes open for the topic or issue outside of school. Did they see it in the news? Can they bring in any newspaper articles that touch on the issue? Did they hear their friends or family talking about the topic, or using the skill they have covered in class?

- If you are already making a wall display based on a topic, you can easily incorporate a 'Link the learning' activity. Provide students with a piece of paper or card with the image of a large paper-clip or link in a chain. Ask them to write on it their idea of how the topic is linked to other subjects or to their lives outside school. Display their ideas around your existing posters, student work or other display material.

Example

Poverty and wealth

Subject: Religious Studies
Level: Key Stage 4

Students studying the guidance of different religions towards wealth, poverty and people's responsibility towards each other identified, among others, the following links to questions in the news, other subjects and their everyday lives:

> *Life link:*
>
> Should I give money to charity, even though I don't get a big allowance?

> *Citizenship and Geography link:*
>
> Does our government have a responsibility to help poorer countries?

> *Life link:*
>
> Should I give money to beggars?

> *Citizenship link:*
>
> Does our government do enough to support less well-off people in our country?

> *Careers and Life link:*
>
> Are there jobs it would be wrong for me to have?

Other titles available in the Starters and Plenaries series:

More Secondary Starters and Plenaries by Mike Gershon
Secondary Starters and Plenaries: English by Johnnie Young
Secondary Starters and Plenaries: History by Mike Gershon

Other titles available from Bloomsbury Education:

How to Survive Your First Year in Teaching by Sue Cowley
Teacher: Mastering the art and craft of teaching by Tom Bennett
Why Are You Shouting At Us? The dos and don'ts of behaviour management by Phil Beadle and John Murphy